ABOUT ISLAND PRESS

Island Press is the only nonprofit organization in the United States whose principal purpose is the publication of books on environmental issues and natural resource management. We provide solutions-oriented information to professionals, public officials, business and community leaders, and concerned citizens who are shaping responses to environmental problems.

Since 1984, Island Press has been the leading provider of timely and practical books that take a multidisciplinary approach to critical environmental concerns. Our growing list of titles reflects our commitment to bringing the best of an expanding body of literature to the environmental community throughout North America and the world.

Support for Island Press is provided by the Agua Fund, The Geraldine R. Dodge Foundation, Doris Duke Charitable Foundation, The Ford Foundation, The William and Flora Hewlett Foundation, The Joyce Foundation, Kendeda Sustainability Fund of the Tides Foundation, The Forrest & Frances Lattner Foundation, The Henry Luce Foundation, The John D. and Catherine T. MacArthur Foundation, The Marisla Foundation, The Andrew W. Mellon Foundation, Gordon and Betty Moore Foundation, The Curtis and Edith Munson Foundation, National Fish and Wildlife Foundation, Oak Foundation, The Overbrook Foundation, The David and Lucile Packard Foundation, Wallace Global Fund, The Winslow Foundation, and other generous donors.

The opinions expressed in this book are those of the author(s) and do not necessarily reflect the views of these foundations.

ABOUT THE LANDSCAPE ARCHITECTURE FOUNDATION

The Landscape Architecture Foundation is a national nonprofit organization whose mission is the preservation, improvement, and enhancement of the environment. LAF accomplishes its mission through information, research, leadership development, and scholarship on sustainable landscape planning and design.

Sustainable land design provides a holistic, systemic way of integrating science, design, and technology to issues at the intersection of land, people, and nature and is relevant to critical issues such as urban revitalization, transportation, public health and safety, affordable housing, cultural identity, and water and air quality.

LAF's purpose is to support design and planning solutions that preserve and conserve natural and cultural resources and create safer, healthier, more livable communities.

ABOUT THE LAND AND COMMUNITY DESIGN CASE STUDY SERIES

The Landscape Architecture Foundation's *Land and Community Design Case Studies* is a series of analytical publications by contemporary scholars and practitioners about topical issues and actual places in which design offers holistic solutions to economic, social, and environmental problems. The goal of the series is to provide a legacy of critical thinking that will advance enlightened planning and development in the classroom, in practice and in policy.

BIODIVERSITY PLANNING AND DESIGN

BIODIVERSITY PLANNING AND DESIGN

SUSTAINABLE PRACTICES

JACK AHERN

ELIZABETH LEDUC

MARY LEE YORK

ISLANDPRESS

WASHINGTON · COVELO · LONDON

© 2006 Island Press

ISLAND PRESS is a trademark of the Center for Resource Economics.

Library of Congress Cataloging-in-Publication Data

Ahern, Jack (John F.)
  Biodiversity planning and design : sustainable practices / Landscape Architecture
Foundation ; Jack Ahern, Elizabeth Leduc, and Mary Lee York.
       p. cm.
  Includes bibliographical references.
  ISBN-13: 978-1-59726-108-1 (cloth : alk. paper)
  ISBN-10: 1-59726-108-4 (cloth : alk. paper)
  ISBN-13: 978-1-59726-109-8 (pbk. : alk. paper)
  ISBN-10: 1-59726-109-2 (pbk. : alk. paper)
 1. Biodiversity--Conservation. 2. Landscape design. 3. Restoration ecology. 4.
Sustainable development. I. Leduc, Elizabeth. II. York, Mary Lee. III. Title.
  QH75.A347 2006
  333.95'16--dc22

                                                    2006021688

Printed on recycled, acid-free paper ♼

Design by Lyle Rosbotham

Manufactured in the United States of America
10 9 8 7 6 5 4 3 2 1

C O N T E N T S

CASE STUDY METHODS AND DESIGN

The research methods used in this study are based on the article "A Case Study Method for Landscape Architecture" (Francis 2001) and Yin's methods (1994) for case study design and analysis. We also consulted the Land and Community Design Case Study Series, jointly published by the Landscape Architecture Foundation (LAF) and Island Press (Francis 2003a, 2003b; Schneider 2003). In this work, a range of case study research methods were used, including structured interviews, document review, project review, field visits, and published literature. To gain a broader perspective on each case, a range of information sources were consulted, including landscape architecture and planning academicians, ecologists and conservation biologists, landscape architect practitioners, and U.S. agency professionals.

This issue-based case study examined the topic of biodiversity from an applications perspective in both public and private landscape architecture and planning practice. Through a cross-case analysis method, the research analyzed strategies and approaches to biodiversity planning, design, restoration, and management. It considered biodiversity across a spectrum from statewide to individual project scales. The cases are presented in a sequence from fine to broad scale, starting with site-based projects in Washington, Massachusetts, and Michigan, and then moving to river basin and statewide planning efforts in Oregon and Florida.

RESEARCH PROCESS

The case study selection and analysis followed several specific steps:
1. Review biodiversity planning and design from multiple perspectives to determine definitions, trends, key questions, and planning and design strategies.
2. Review literature on biodiversity and apply it for constructing research propositions to structure the case study design, protocol, and analysis.
3. Select projects to represent (a) a diversity of scales (alpha, beta, gamma), (b) multiple geographic contexts in the United States (Washington, Massachusetts, Michigan, Oregon, and Florida), (c) significant involvement of landscape archi-

tects and planners, and (d) projects that represent innovative work of high professional and academic standards.

4. Identify key individuals, organizations and applications for in-depth analysis of each project.
5. Gather evidence (conduct interviews, visit projects, literature review, and applications research).
6. Analyze the case study evidence, and prepare a draft report for review and comment.
7. Prepare the final case study, including illustrations.

CASE STUDY PROPOSITIONS

Preliminary research on biodiversity planning and design helped us to articulate four research propositions. These propositions were designed to reflect key theoretical issues and to raise important "how" and "why" questions about biodiversity planning and design. The propositions, listed below, were addressed in each case study and are discussed in the concluding chapter.

1. Biodiversity planning is in demand in rural, suburban, and urban areas.
2. Landscape architects and planners will play a larger role in biodiversity planning and restoration ecology as nondegraded habitat becomes scarce.
3. Biodiversity goals that are explicitly part of a project's goal or design process are more likely to be achieved.
4. Integrating biological and ecological information with the planning and design process will contribute to a better balance between land use and the natural environment and will increase public awareness of biodiversity's value to humans.

INTRODUCTION: BIODIVERSITY PLANNING AND DESIGN

The state of biodiversity is of increasing concern around the world. Considerable agreement exists among scientists that habitat loss and degradation are among the leading causes of global biodiversity decline. Renowned entomologist and champion of biodiversity awareness E. O. Wilson (1988, 3) claims: "Overall we are locked into a race. We must hurry to acquire the knowledge on which a wise policy of conservation and development can be based for centuries to come."

If habitat loss is the leading cause of biodiversity decline, it follows that planning and design will be essential in any viable solution by directly conserving, protecting, or managing landscapes and habitats. Planners set policy and make plans to organize land use to meet multiple goals. Landscape architects create designs that are realized in physical form, affecting protection, change, and restoration of land and habitat. Landscape architects and planners engage biodiversity by working independently or in interdisciplinary teams that include conservation biologists, restoration ecologists, and natural and social scientists. Some of these teams have very successfully addressed biodiversity across a range of scales and geographical contexts.

As part of its case study series, the Landscape Architecture Foundation (LAF) sponsored this issue-based research into how landscape architects and planners have addressed biodiversity in their work. This case study undertook to learn how biodiversity fits with other goals in professional planning and design work; the role(s) of landscape architects and planners in interdisciplinary teams; and strategies for moving forward with biodiversity planning and design when faced with uncertainty and incomplete knowledge. The study includes five biodiversity planning and design projects, arranged into a comparative, issue-based case study representing a range of scales and geographic locations across the United States. The projects include the following:

- The Woodland Park Zoo's long-range plan, by Jones & Jones, Architects and Landscape Architects, in Seattle, Washington.
- A storm water management and wetland restoration project by Carol R. Johnson and Associates in Devens, Massachusetts.

- The Crosswinds Marsh Wetland Mitigation project, in Wayne County, Michigan, by the Smith Group/JJR of Ann Arbor, Michigan.
- The Willamette River Basin Study in Oregon, by University of Oregon landscape architect David Hulse and colleagues.
- The Florida Statewide Greenways System Planning Project, by the University of Florida Department of Landscape Architecture.

Our research found that biodiversity planning best succeeds when it is integrated with other goals, including environmental education, environmental impact mitigation, and regulatory compliance. Achieving multiple goals requires an interdisciplinary approach, and planners and designers often excel in leading such teams. Landscape architects and planners offer the ability to synthesize and visualize complex information, a familiarity with construction processes, skills in facilitating public participation, and expertise in implementing and managing projects. Additionally, the case study found that, although important, biodiversity is often a secondary or minor project goal in planning and design projects. It becomes more important in broad-scale, public policy-related projects and when mandated by regulatory and permitting agencies.

Data for planning and designing biodiversity projects are often incomplete for explicitly supporting planning and design decisions—an inherent problem related to the site- and species-specific nature of the data required. Despite the lack of good data, however, monitoring has rarely been conducted, due mostly to cost and convenience. This limits the ongoing involvement of landscape architects and planners in the projects they conceive, design, and build and thus to learn if the intended results were achieved. The lack of monitoring misses opportunities to (1) contribute new knowledge to science, (2) afford planners and designers the chance to expand their interdisciplinary collaboration with scientists and decision makers, and (3) "to learn by doing" to develop and refine planning strategies and design responses to address biodiversity more effectively.

Biodiversity is implicit in virtually all of the work of planners and landscape architects, and many signs point toward increased global interest and support for biodiversity planning. Both disciplines—planning and landscape architecture—include principles guiding the treatment of the natural environment in the ethical codes put forth by their professional societies. Landscape architects are expected to uphold values of environmental stewardship, especially as described in section ES1.13 in the American Society of Landscape Architects' (ASLA) Code of Environmental Ethics: "The principles of land use planning and design and the principles of wildlife habitat protection should be integrated to promote the enhancement, protection, and management of landscapes that promote wildlife" (American Society of Landscape Architects 2000, 1).

Similarly, the American Planning Association outlines its "Ethical Principles in Planning" to guide the behavior of both certified planners and all other working planners. Included in these principles is the statement that planners must "strive to protect the integrity of the natural environment" (American Planning Association 1992,

1). Biodiversity planning and design are central issues for the Society of Ecological Restoration International, which states the following as part of its mission: "to promote ecological restoration as a means of sustaining the diversity of life on Earth and reestablishing an ecologically healthy relationship between nature and culture" (Society for Ecological Restoration International 2004).

Biodiversity represents a significant growth opportunity for planning and design professionals. To become more active players, landscape architects and planners need to: become more familiar with the issues, terminology, and methods for biodiversity planning and design; understand the complex issue of representative species selection and how to apply a method in the context of species/habitat associations and ecological models; and to develop advanced skills for leading interdisciplinary teams. By examining how planners and designers have been involved in five specific projects in the United States and by identifying areas of strength and points of weakness, this study seeks to identify specific ways these professionals can participate in and contribute to biodiversity conservation. The study is intended to not only encourage design and planning professionals to take a more active role in projects that involve biodiversity issues but also to better inform them about biodiversity and conservation efforts in general.

DEFINITIONS OF BIODIVERSITY

Biodiversity has many definitions in the current literature written by independent researchers, government agencies, and international organizations. The differences among the definitions emphasize the complexity of the issue. Some include detailed spatial or temporal considerations, whereas others are quite simple. For example, the Keystone Center (1991, 2) describes biodiversity as "the variety of life and its processes," while biologist B. A. Wilcox (1982, 640) calls it "the variety of life forms, the ecological roles they perform, and the genetic diversity they contain." These simple definitions recognize that both the quantity of species and the ecological processes that affect those species are important. Conservation biologists R. F. Noss and A. Y. Cooperrider (1994, 5) extend the Keystone Center's definition to say: "Biodiversity is the variety of life and its processes. It includes the variety of living organisms, the genetic differences among them, the communities and ecosystems in which they occur, and the ecological and evolutionary processes that keep them functioning, yet ever changing and adapting."

Similarly, the U.S. National Biological Information Infrastructure (NBII), an organization composed of a wide array of federal, state, international, nongovernmental, academic, and industry partners, states that "biodiversity or biological diversity is the sum total of the variety of life and its interactions and can be subdivided into 1) genetic diversity, 2) species diversity, and 3) ecological or ecosystem diversity" (NBI I 2003). In 1992 the World Resources Institute, the World Conservation Union (otherwise known as the IUCN, or International Union for Conservation of Nature and Natural Resources), and the United Nations Environment Programme (UNEP) produced a joint publication, *Global Biodiversity Strategy,* in which biodiversity is defined as "the variability among living organisms from all sources, including, *inter alia*, terrestrial, marine and other aquatic ecosystems and the ecological complexes of which they are part; this includes diversity within species, between species and of ecosystems" (WRI, 1992). *Global Biodiversity Strategy* further characterizes these three categories:

1. Genetic, or alpha, diversity is concerned with the variation of genes within species, including separate populations of the same species or genetic disparity within populations.
2. Species, or beta, diversity refers to the variety of species within a region, while species diversity can be measured in many ways; the number of species in an area, or species richness, is often used. Species diversity is also thought of in terms of taxonomic diversity, which considers the relationship of one species to another.
3. Ecosystem, or gamma, diversity refers to numbers of species in a particular location, the ecological functions of the species, the manner in which the composition of the species varies within a region, the associations of species in particular areas, and the processes within and between these ecosystems. Ecosystem diversity extends to the landscape and biome level.

One of the first scientists to address the issue of scale when measuring species richness was noted ecologist Robert Whittaker, who suggested thinking about species diversity in terms of alpha, beta, and gamma levels: alpha diversity referred to the species in a small, well-defined area, such as a study plot; beta diversity addressed the diversity of species between habitats, such as along a gradient; and gamma diversity was a tally of the number of species over landscapes or vast geographic areas (Whittaker 1975). Likewise, landscape ecologist Sheila Peck (1998) suggests that biodiversity can be characterized according to four different levels of biological organization: landscape, community, population, and genetic.

Some organizations and researchers include temporal and evolutionary aspects of biodiversity in their definitions. For instance, the broad definition put forth by The Nature Conservancy (TNC) and the Association for Biodiversity Information in their joint project *Precious Heritage: The Status of Biodiversity in the United States* not only includes references to genes, species, and ecosystems but expands to say that "biodiversity also encompasses the processes—both ecological and evolutionary—that allow life on Earth to continue adapting and evolving" (Groves et al. 2000, 7). This temporal component also surfaces in Peck's definition of biodiversity as "not only the range of variation that can be seen today, but that which is expressed over a period of time" (Peck 1998, 17).

The definitions above show three principal similarities: (1) biodiversity exists and needs to be understood at multiple scales, (2) biodiversity is inseparable from its physical environment, and (3) biodiversity is integral with ecological processes. For this study, we have integrated these similarities into the following working definition: *Biodiversity is the totality, over time, of genes, species, and ecosystems in an ecosystem or region, including the ecosystem structure and function that supports and sustains life.*

THE STATUS OF BIODIVERSITY— MEASUREMENT AND TRENDS

Whether or not such issues as spatial or temporal contexts or accompanying ecological processes are addressed, a general consensus exists that, at the very least, the concept of biodiversity rests on baseline knowledge of the number of species that exist on earth. This itself is a controversial topic; estimates of the number of species span orders of magnitude, ranging widely according to the method of calculation and the data used. E. O. Wilson (1988) suggests that the true number of species ranges anywhere from 5 to 30 million. In 1982, Terry L. Erwin's (1982) method of gassing and collecting insects from select trees in a Panamanian rain forest lead him to propose that, worldwide, there are 30 million species of tropical arthropods alone. Basing his estimates on the assumption that an inverse relationship exists between the numbers of species and body size, University of Oxford zoologist Robert M. May (1988) estimated global species richness to be between 10 and 50 million species. In 1995, the United Nations Environment Programme (UNEP) estimated that there are 13.6 million species on earth (Hammond 1995). This figure—which is very close to that of 13.4 million species proposed by Nigel Stork (1999) for the "Living Planet in Crisis" conference sponsored by the American Museum of Natural History in 1995—is currently considered an acceptable working estimate.

Ironically, biologists have the least information about the groups that are most common, such as insects. Currently, most "named" species are vertebrate and plant species, while the number of insect species is yet unknown. The best estimate of the total number of insect species on earth is 8.75 million, while only about 1.025 million (12 percent) have been named (see Table 1.1). In contrast, 4,650, or 97 percent, of the estimated 4,800 total number of mammal species have been named (Gibbs 2001).

	Estimated Worldwide Total	Total Number Currently Named	Percent
All Species	8,750,000	1,025,000	12
Mammals	4,800	4,650	97

Table 1.1. Named vs. Unnamed Global Species. *Source: Gibbs 2001.*

In response to such uncertainties, efforts to catalog species diversity are ongoing at global, national, and regional scales. On a global scale, the World Conservation Union has an initiative to evaluate the status of more than one hundred thousand species in a five year period (World Conservation Union–IUCN 2000). This organization has been working for forty years to assess the global conservation status of species in order to draw attention to taxa threatened with extinction. One product of this assessment is the Red Book program, formed to reduce global extinction rates by making an index of biodiversity loss worldwide and by identifying species at the highest risk (World Conservation Union–IUCN 2001). By comparing the results from the year 2000 Red List of Endangered Species with those from the 1996 Red List, the World Conservation Union found that the severity of the extinction crisis was actually worse than had been

Table 1.2. Percentages of Global Species That Are Currently Threatened.

Source: World Conservation Union–IUCN 2000.

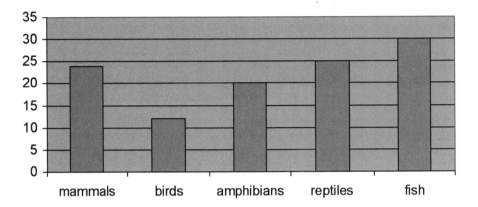

IUCN Percentages of Global Species that are Threatened

previously estimated and that the populations of many species were declining rapidly (World Conservation Union–IUCN 2000). In total, the World Conservation Union considers approximately eleven thousand species of plants and animals to be threatened. Specifically, their results show that 24 percent of mammal species, 12 percent of birds, 20 percent of amphibians, 25 percent of reptiles, and 30 percent of fish face a high risk of becoming extinct in the near future (Table 1.2) (World Conservation Union–IUCN 2000, 1–2). Other global efforts include the Global Biodiversity Information Facility (GBIF) and Species 2000, two initiatives joined to build a comprehensive Internet database of species (Species 2000, 2002).

Clearly, we do not know the total number of all species on earth, and by the best estimates we have named only a small fraction of the existing biodiversity. At a global level, most expert accounts indicate that we are facing significant decline of species in some of the most species-rich segments of the world. Compounding this problem is the fact that most of the biodiversity in the world exists in the tropics, in developing countries with expanding populations and scant resources that are unable to deal with cataloging and conserving species. Undoubtedly, future global policy and planning measures must address this challenge through continued research, conservation, and development of sustainable, economical conservation policies.

Despite its mostly temperate climate, the United States ranks rather high in terms of global diversity. According to the Massachusetts Executive Office of Environmental Affairs (2001), the United States ranks number one in total percentage of global species for freshwater mussels, snails, and crayfish. The U.S. also contains 9 percent of worldwide mammal species and 7 percent of flowering plants. Many national efforts are underway to inventory and assess the status of biodiversity in the U.S. As a result of the 1973 Endangered Species Act, the Threatened and Endangered Species System (TESS) of the U.S. Department of Fish and Wildlife Service lists species considered to be endangered or threatened in the United States. The database currently lists 509 species of animals, with twenty-five proposed to be added to the list, and 740 species of plants, with ten additional species proposed (U.S. Fish and Wildlife Service 2002).

The Natural Heritage Network is another national inventory effort, a result of the cooperation of state agencies from across the country, The Nature Conservancy, and the Association for Biodiversity Information. The Heritage Network operates in all fifty states and has recently expanded to encompass several other countries in the Western Hemisphere. Its database assesses the status of more than thirty thousand of the estimated two hundred thousand species in the United States and indicates that roughly one-third of these are of conservation concern (Master et al. 2000, 101) (Figure 1.1).

Working at the regional level, the All Taxa Biodiversity Inventory (ATBI), an initiative in the Great Smoky Mountains, recently discovered 115 previously unknown species in an eighteen-month period (All Taxa Biodiversity Inventory 2002). In Massachusetts the Natural Heritage and Endangered Species Program, a collaboration between the Executive Office of Environmental Affairs and TNC, has created the Massachusetts Biological and Conservation Database, a compilation of more than ten thousand records for some six hundred different species in the state. Results show that in the last two hundred and fifty years, seven vertebrate species and an estimated sixty to seventy species of plants have been extirpated from Massachusetts (Massachusetts Executive Office of Environmental Affairs 2001).

Thus, while the United States enjoys the luxury of having many different organizations

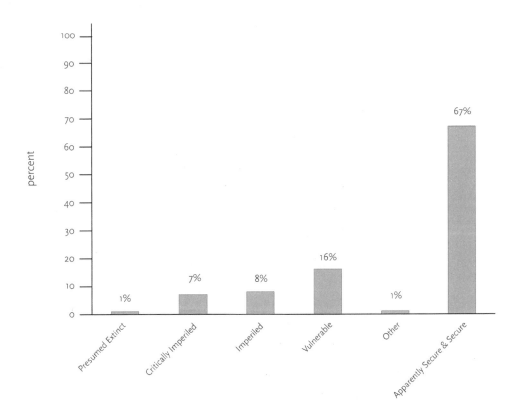

Figure 1.1. The Nature Conservancy rankings for native U.S. fauna and flora. See *Nature Conservancy conservation status rank* in the glossary for explanations of ranking categories.

Source: Master et al. 2000.

working at different scales to assess and conserve biodiversity, many challenges still exist. According to the U.S. Department of Agriculture, roughly 70 percent of the land area of the United States is privately owned and a significant number (nearly one fourth) of imperiled and endangered species reside on these lands. Furthermore, a comparison of concentrations of threatened biodiversity with concentrations of the U.S. human population reveals an alarming degree of overlap (Groves et al. 2000). Future decisions about how to conserve biodiversity will involve complex negotiations with the needs and interests of humans, including consideration of the biodiversity of urban and suburban areas.

Although a general consensus exists that the rate of extinction has been increasing, uncertainty remains regarding the actual magnitude of this rate. According to Robert May, the extinction rate has accelerated during the past one hundred years to roughly one thousand times what it was before humans appeared on earth. He explains that various lines of argument "suggest a speeding up by a further factor of 10 over the next century or so. . . . And that puts us squarely on the breaking edge of the sixth great wave of extinction in the history of life on earth" (May, cited by Gibbs 2001, 42). Citing statistics by the World Conservation Union, May (1988) predicts that extinction rates will rise twelve to fifty-five times over the next three centuries. In 1993, Smith et al. extrapolated from current recorded extinction rates to predict an alarming extinction rate of 50 percent for some taxonomic groups, such as birds and mammals, within three to four hundred years. Even more extreme estimates of 8 to 11 percent species loss per decade were suggested by researchers in the 1980s (Lovejoy 1980; Raven 1988).

Many of these scientists based their estimates on the species-area theory offered by MacArthur and Wilson (1967), which predicts that a 90 percent reduction in habitat area will result in a loss of half of the total species in that area. E.O. Wilson suggests that species loss will continue until the human population stops increasing; he refers to the present day as the "bottleneck" period "because we have to pass through that scramble for remaining resources in order to get to an era, perhaps sometime in the twenty-second century, of declining human population. Our goal is to carry as much of the biodiversity through as possible" (quoted in Gibbs 2001, 49).

Some scientists, however, disagree with these estimates. Brown and Brown (1992) noted that, although Atlantic rain forests had been reduced to 12 percent of their original extent, the 50 percent extinction rate estimated by species-area predictions did not seem to be holding up. Others have noted that it is very difficult to precisely identify when the last specimen of a given species has died (Ehrlich and Wilson 1991; Mawdsley and Stork 1995). It may take years for the cumulative factors affecting extinction to draw the final blow (Heywood et al. 1994). These species are therefore condemned to certain extinction, though they may survive for several decades before becoming extinct.

By far the greatest challenge to the startling extinction predictions from biologists over the years has come from Danish statistician Bjørn Lomborg. In his book *The Skeptical Environmentalist*, Lomborg charges that reports of the decline of biodiversity have been greatly exaggerated and that environmentalists have ignored evidence that tropical deforestation has not taken the predicted toll on species diversity (Lomborg 2001). The scientific community, however disregards his extremely conservative estimate of 0.15 percent of species loss per decade on the basis that he is not a biological scientist and that he relies on poor data (Gibbs 2001, 43).

At the very least, scientists agree that the rate of extinction is increasing above what would be considered normal background levels and that, as a result, global biodiversity is declining. Ongoing efforts to name and catalog species will improve our understanding of these losses and what can be done to prevent or slow them. However, while the naming and describing of species continues, scientists and other conservation professionals must also make decisions about how to conserve existing biodiversity with limited information and resources. What approach should they take? How can they decide which species to conserve? How many individuals are needed to sustain a viable population for a given species in a region? Indeed, how can they assess population trends?

STRATEGIES FOR ASSESSING AND CONSERVING BIODIVERSITY

Landscape architects and planners must rely on the expertise of biologists to conduct biodiversity assessments, and it is important that they understand the pertinent concepts and terminology so they can collaborate effectively. Methods to assess and conserve biodiversity fall into two broad categories: reactive strategies, which are undertaken once a problem or issue has been identified, and proactive strategies, undertaken before a problem arises. Biodiversity plans that integrate both are likely to be more successful.

Biodiversity is commonly evaluated by either an "endangered species" reactive approach that addresses species that are already in trouble; or a "hot spot" proactive approach that focuses on protecting geographical areas with high concentrations of biodiversity. Historically in North America, species conservation methods were aimed at preserving single species that had some perceived value to humankind and whose declining numbers needed to be managed to ensure the species' future use by humans. Desirable species (such as deer and caribou) were managed, while undesirable species (such as wolves) were pushed to the brink of extinction. These early efforts tended to focus on large-game vertebrates that could be exploited for their meat or hides. Gradually, aided by the passage of the Endangered Species Act of 1973 (the ESA), the scope of species to be conserved expanded to include invertebrates, plants, and other historically undervalued species (Noss and Cooperrider 1994). Under the ESA, vulnerable species are those in danger of becoming extinct or those federally listed as being threatened or endangered (TES) (Feinsinger 2001). This vulnerable species approach has several drawbacks:

- Until recently, it has focused on large vertebrates to the exclusion of plants and invertebrates.

- This fine filter, single-species approach cannot possibly keep tabs on the vast numbers of species in the world.
- Historically, this approach has addressed direct threats to species survival, such as poaching and hunting—a focus that has become increasingly misguided as habitat loss has eclipsed direct killing as the major threat to species.
- Most single-species efforts are reactive, coming into play only after a given species is imperiled (Noss and Cooperrider 1994).

The endangered species approach came into fundamental conflict with development activities, leading to multispecies habitat conservation plans that attempted to negotiate a reasonable compromise between conservation and development, informed by species biology and development alternatives, while operating within the legal guidelines of the ESA. To the purist, habitat conservation plans represent an unacceptable weakening of the ESA; to others, they provide a model for sustainable "balancing" of conservation and development in which serious consideration is granted to biodiversity (Beatley 1994).

Alternatively, a hotspot approach is more strategic and proactive in that it entails the protection of areas that help conserve overall diversity before the quality of the ecosystems and species within those areas degrades entirely. Generally, hotspots are high in species richness and endemic species (those species found only in a single location in the world). Hotspots may also be determined by the degree of threat to the area. For example, Conservation International, a U.S.-based, international nonprofit organization, uses a hotspot approach as its central strategy for preserving biodiversity. It has identified twenty-five hotspots worldwide, where it concentrates its efforts. According to Russell A. Mittermeier, president of Conservation International: "The hotspots strategy makes the extinction crisis more manageable by enabling us to prioritize and target conservation investments in order to have the greatest impact" (Conservation International 2002).

Another example of the hotspot approach is the National Gap Analysis Program (GAP), conducted by the Biological Resource Division of the U.S. Geological Survey. It is used to analyze how well native animal species and natural plant communities are represented in the network of currently protected lands. In the GAP analysis, "gaps" are areas in which particular species or natural communities are not adequately represented in currently protected lands. GAP assessment classifies lands into four management classes, which range from permanently protected with natural disturbance regimes (class 1) to unprotected areas with extensive human changes allowed to existing ecosystems and plant communities (class 4) (Jennings 2000). When "gaps" are identified, they may be targeted for acquisition or for alternative management approaches. GAP is a type of hotspot approach in which both ecological processes and species distribution are examined to determine which areas should receive protection before they become vulnerable. A stated goal of the project is "to ensure that all ecosystems and areas rich in species diversity are represented adequately in biodiversity management areas" (Scott et al. 1993, 1).

GAP analysis is a habitat-association method of biodiversity assessment. In GAP, given habitat types are correlated with species needs and preferences (identified in the literature) and then used to predict where those species could potentially exist. GAP information is then verified through field checks. This is a coarse filter approach in which large, mappable vegetation units are presumed to support a wide array of species (Scott et al. 1993; Jennings 2000). Vegetation is mapped using satellite images, and distributions of native animal species are mapped using museum or agency specimen collection records, known general ranges, and habitat associations. The resulting geographic information systems (GIS) maps are then overlaid with maps of land management areas to identify "gaps" and to focus conservation and land acquisitions efforts. Since its inception in 1988, GAP mapping has been completed for the forty-eight contiguous states, supporting not only gap planning but other multipurpose statewide and regional planning activities, including greenway planning. Jennings (2000) predicts that human activities will be more explicitly integrated with GAP analysis in the future, leading to the development of a comprehensive biodiversity decision support system.

Another coarse filter, proactive conservation and planning approach that attempts to work at regional scales and over broader time periods is the ecoregion approach used by the World Wildlife Fund (WWF), based on the work of James Omernick of the U.S. Environmental Protection Agency (EPA) and Robert Bailey of the U.S. Forest Service (Stein, Kutner, and Adams 2000). Ecoregions are broad regions of land or water that include "geographically distinct assemblage of natural communities," which contain many of the same ecological processes and species, exist under similar environmental conditions, and depend on ecological interactions for long-term survival (Dinerstein et al. 2000, 13). The WWF has identified more than two hundred ecoregions and uses them to set conservation priorities. Ecoregions simplify landscapes to reveal underlying patterns. To address biodiversity with a more fine-grained, intermediate-scale approach, The Nature Conservancy and the National Heritage Network rely instead on mapping ecological communities which are assemblages of species that exist together in the same areas and whose life processes are potentially interrelated (McPeek and Miller 1996).

Selecting species for biodiversity planning presents a great dilemma: to be truly inclusive many species need to be considered, yet there is rarely enough species-specific knowledge, information, or time to support this type of inclusive approach. As the number of species considered increases, so too do the time and cost of planning. In response to this dilemma, biodiversity planners often use representative, or indicator, species. An indicator species is a species whose status provides information on the overall condition of an ecosystem and of other species in that ecosystem. Indicator species flag changes in biotic or abiotic conditions. They reflect the quality of and changes in environmental conditions as well as aspects of community composition (Heywood and Watson 1995).

Biodiversity planners commonly think of the term *indicator species* as synonymous with *target species*. However, some experts contend that target species are often chosen more for their value in conservation politics than for their validity as true biological indicators (Landres et al. 1988; Noss 1990; Feinsinger 2001; Storch and Bissonette 2003). In this way, target species are used reactively. In addition, problems can arise in determining what species should serve as indicators; there appears to be little consensus in the literature regarding methods of selection for indicator fauna (Hilty and Merenlender 2000). Table 1.3 provides a list of common methods for selecting species for biodiversity planning.

The selection process for indicators is critical and should consider sampling techniques and sample sizes, scale, environmental stressors, and appropriateness of the species as a surrogate for a larger community of species. Reed Noss (1990) explains the need to select indicators at different levels of organization and outlines variables for cataloging, observing, and assessing biodiversity at regional, ecosystem, species, and genetic scales. Indicators may be positive, in that they are expected to correlate positively with ecological integrity or biodiversity, or negative, in that their presence indicates a degradation of ecosystem health. Most ecologists suggest that a single species should never be used as a positive indicator for biodiversity planning; rather, multispecies indicators that range across spatial scales should be used. However, when using negative indicators, one may be sufficient. An example is the bacteria *Escherichia coli*, the presence of which always indicates poor water quality, usually originating from improperly treated human waste.

The use of target species is generally reactive, focusing on the species itself but not generally on the biota interacting with that species. Targets commonly receive attention because they are in some danger of extinction. Indicators, on the other hand, are more proactive because they are chosen to act as "signals" that change before change actually occurs. Finally, ecosystem patterns, processes, or relationships are receiving more attention as indicators to biodiversity, as "species based approaches have been criticized on the grounds that they do not provide whole-landscape solutions to conservation problems" (Lambeck 1997, 850).

Because the design of a project may depend on the type of biodiversity strategy used, landscape architects must consult with ecologists before any planning or design process begins. We will now examine why landscape architects and planners should acknowledge biodiversity in their planning and design efforts.

WHY SHOULD BIODIVERSITY BE IMPORTANT TO LANDSCAPE ARCHITECTS AND PLANNERS?

All societies depend on biodiversity and biological resources either directly or indirectly. Humans rely directly on the diversity of life on earth as a source of air (plants produce oxygen through photosynthesis), fuel, fiber, medicines and, most importantly, for food. We also depend on microbes and scavengers to break down wastes, recycle nutrients, and replenish our soils (Miller et al. 1985). Placing a value on biodiversity is

1. Charismatic species—aesthetically appealing and likely to generate sympathy among the general population. Examples include butterflies, *Lepidoptera* spp., wolves, *Canis lupis*; giant pandas, *Ailuropoda melanoleuca*; and orchids family Orchidae. These families and species are often marketable and used in advertising campaigns (Feinsinger 2001).

2. Flagship species—popular and charismatic species. They attract popular support for conservation and often help to spearhead a conservation effort in a particular landscape. Vertebrate species—such as the northern spotted owl *Strix occidentalis*, in the Pacific Northwest, or the Florida panther *Puma concolor coryi*, are most often considered flagship species (Simberloff 1998; Schrader-Frechette and McCoy 1993).

3. Umbrella species—species that require large areas of habitat in order to maintain viable populations. The protection of their habitat protects the habitat and populations of numerous other species within the range, like an umbrella. These species have been described as an efficient means of meeting the needs of all species without having to monitor every individual species, because they tend to function as "coarse filters" (Wilcove 1993). Umbrella species are useful for prioritizing habitat remnants for conservation or other land uses (Fleishman, Murphy, and Brussard 2000). The grizzly bear *Ursus arctos*, and the American bison, *Bison bison*, are examples.

4. Focal—species whose requirements for persistence include attributes that must be present for a landscape to meet the needs of most of the species in the given area. This is essentially an extension of the umbrella species concept. When dealing with multispecies management, professionals group species according to threats and then select the most sensitive species for each threat to act as the focal species. This species then determines maximum acceptable levels of threat (Lambeck 1997). The hooded robin in Australia, *Melanodryas cucullata*, has been used as a focal species (Freudenberger 1999).

5. Vulnerable species—species in danger of becoming extinct. When the U.S. government recognizes a species, vulnerability because of its advanced state, that species is considered to be threatened or endangered (Feinsinger 2001). The bald eagle, *Haliaeetus leucocephalus*, is a well-known example of a vulnerable species.

6. Keystone species—species whose impact on ecosystems is disproportionately large relative to their abundance. They often function in close association with landscape processes and disturbances. One example is the beaver, *Castor canadensis*, whose engineering effects on the landscape are integral to shaping ecosystems (Power et al. 1996).

7. Economically valuable species that are needed by local consumers or that hold value in the commercial marketplace (Feinsinger 2001). The caribou, *Rangifer tarandus*, is a good example in this category.

8. Species guild—a group of species that uses a particular resource in similar ways. One example is all the bird species that make their nests in holes in tree trunks (Croonquist and Brooks 1991)—cavity nesting species such as the American kestrel *Falco sparverius*; barred owl *Strix varia*; hairy woodpecker *Picoides villosus*; and Eastern bluebird *Sialia sialis*.

Table 1.3. Examples of Species Selection Approaches for Biodiversity Planning.

difficult because the many ecological services and functions performed by biodiversity, such as climate regulation, do not have explicit markets and are difficult to quantify. Often, the aesthetic or moral values associated with biodiversity are not explicitly acknowledged in ecological or economic assessments (Organisation for Economic

Co-operation and Development 2002). Today, justification of the importance of conserving biodiversity falls into three main categories:

1. The vast repository of genetic information stored in the diversity of the earth's organisms provides a buffer against disease and famine because it holds the building blocks for biotechnological discoveries (e.g., future foods and medicines).
2. Ecosystems provide services to the earth (e.g., filtering carbon dioxide), and we do not yet understand the full extent or economic value of the possible services.
3. Humans have a moral obligation to preserve the balance of life on earth (Gibbs 2001). Ehrenfeld's "Noah principle" makes this point elegantly: "They [species] should be conserved because they exist and because this existence is itself but the present expression of a continued historical process of immense antiquity and majesty. Long-standing existence in nature is deemed to carry with it the unimpeachable right to continued existence" (quoted in Beatley, 1994, 9).

The state of biodiversity is currently fragile and is heavily influenced by land use decisions. Understanding biodiversity and its functions is important to landscape architects and planners because, by definition, planning and design change spatial configurations, ecological patterns, and the processes linked to these—often unintentionally. For example, most road construction causes habitat fragmentation, disrupts hydrological processes, subjects species to roadkill, and introduces pollutants and people into areas that were previously inaccessible (Forman et al. 2003). Additionally, listing biodiversity protection as one objective among many may help landscape architects and planners to garner a wider range of support and to form partnerships that facilitate other efforts in landscape planning, such as water resource planning, agriculture and wood production, and community and cultural adhesion (Forman 1995).

Human land use and development are quickly fragmenting and decreasing the amount of available open space suitable for habitat. Many biologists consider habitat fragmentation to be the "single greatest threat to biological diversity" (Noss 1991, 27). As the human population increases, the amount of land altered by the cultural landscape also increases. A case in point: in the past fifty years, the human population in the state of Massachusetts has increased by 28 percent while the developed land area has increased by 200 percent. In fact, this state loses forty-four acres (17.8 hectares) of land *each day* to development (Massachusetts Executive Office of Environmental Affairs 2001).

In the book *Once There Were Greenfields: How Urban Sprawl is Undermining America's Environment, Economy and Social Fabric*, authors Benfield, Raimi, and Chen (1999), of the Natural Resources Defense Council, cite the following statistics: from 1995 to 2020, Maryland is expected to witness the conversion of more of its land into housing than that which occurred over the past 350 years. Likewise, from 1970 to 1990, Chicago experienced a 74 percent increase in the metropolitan region's commercial and industrial land use, which is eighteen times greater than the population increase. This acceleration of land consumption is occurring even in areas experiencing a decrease in population: in the past thirty years, the population of greater Cleveland has decreased by 11 percent while urban land use has increased by 33 percent.

Scientists have tried to quantify the direct statistical relationship between loss of habitat area and loss of species. As stated earlier, species-area theories assert that eliminating 90 percent of a given habitat area cuts the number of species in half. Though this figure is hotly debated in the scientific community, it is widely acknowledged that the fragmentation and conversion of habitat to urbanized and agricultural lands generally reduces biodiversity of native species (Mac et al. 1998).

Habitat destruction affects not only the quantity of species but also the quality of those species that survive. Species are disproportionately affected depending on the size of their habitat and where their habitat exists in relation to the altered land. Generalists or edge species, which are able to survive in a variety of habitats, are less likely to suffer from habitat loss and fragmentation than specialist species, which require unique pockets of habitat. Likewise, all species have a minimum area point—how large a given habitat area must be in order for a viable population to survive. Different species or groups will have different minimum area requirements and thus will be affected differently by habitat fragmentation and loss (Forman 1995).

Specifically, fragmentation of the landscape affects habitat size, shape, and distance from other areas of suitable habitat. Those organisms dependent on a particular habitat size or distance (or both) from the edge of their habitat are pressured by the increase of "edge" environment that accompanies fragmentation. This, in turn, affects species diversity directly and indirectly. These effects include changes in predator-prey relationships, alteration of seed dispersal mechanisms, and nest parasitism. Fragmentation also affects abiotic factors, such as hydrologic regimes, mineral nutrient cycles, radiation balance, wind patterns, disturbance regimes, and soil movements. These, in turn, can affect species movement and survival. In particular, forests and the species (including humans) living both within these habitats and in surrounding areas are negatively affected by fragmentation. Normally, forests play a large role in protecting the quality of water by protecting aquifers from evaporation, by monitoring stream network connectivity, and by acting as floodplains (Forman 1995).

One specific consideration relevant in terms of biodiversity for environmental designers and planners is habitat composition, which affects the populations and communities relying on different types of land cover. An example is the decline since the 1950s of certain New England bird and mammal populations commonly linked to young forest habitats that are maturing, thereby losing their brushy quality (Kittredge and O'Shea 1999, 34).

A second aspect of species composition that can be affected by the actions and decisions of landscape architects is the use of native versus exotic species in designed landscapes. Introducing nonindigenous species to an area can disrupt population, community, and ecosystem structure and function (Vitousek 1988; Drake et al. 1989). Certain exotic invasives outcompete native species, leading to habitat degradation and potentially to a monoculture. Some of the most harmful invasive species—such as kudzu

(*Pueraria lobata*), water hyacinth (*Eichhornia crassipes*), and Asian bittersweet (*Celastrus orbiculatus*)—were intentionally introduced to solve agriculture or soil management problems. Other invasives were introduced unintentionally through such means as ballast water in ships, transport on military vehicles, and cut flowers (Mac et al. 1998). One example of the effect of invasive plants is the success of purple loosestrife (*Lythrum salicaria*), which accidentally arrived in the dry ballast in cargo holds of ships and is now overrunning river floodplains and coastal and inland marshes throughout the northeastern United States (Wilcove et al. 2000). As the public's appetite for exotic landscape plants and animals has increased, many of these organisms have been unintentionally released into the wild in the United States, disrupting native ecosystems.

Human land use has significantly affected biodiversity through habitat change, loss, and fragmentation. For example, of the list of federally listed species under the ESA and those listed as species at risk by the Natural Heritage Central Databases, habitat loss has affected 90 percent of bird species, 94 percent of fish, 87 percent of amphibians, 97 percent of reptiles, and 89 percent of mammals in the U.S. (Wilcove et al. 2000). The goal now should be to more deeply understand this threat and determine ways to decrease its negative effects.

CONCLUSION

To be seen as leaders in the environmental community, landscape architects and planners cannot afford to dismiss the importance of biodiversity. They must recognize that the elements of biodiversity planning are interdependent and cannot be addressed in isolation. For example, decisions concerning types of linkages used to increase connectivity for a particular animal species may also increase the connectivity for the dispersal of an invasive plant. By acknowledging these connections, landscape architects and planners can potentially protect and restore biodiversity. Clearly, landscape architects and planners working in both the public and private sectors could have a large effect on the future of any unprotected landscape. They must examine how well they are able to adhere to the overarching priorities of sustainability in their daily work. The current state of biodiversity calls for a reevaluation of ethics and a return to Aldo Leopold's concept of human beings as stewards of the land, safeguarding resources for future generations:

> All ethics so far evolved rest upon a single premise: that the individual is a member of a community of interdependent parts. His instincts prompt him to compete for his place in that community, but his ethics prompt him also to cooperate (perhaps in order that there may be a place to compete for). The land ethic simply enlarges the boundaries of the community to include soils, waters, plants, and animals, or collectively: the land. (Leopold 1949, 203–4)

U.S. Environmental Protection Agency (U.S.EPA)

http://www.epa.gov/

The U.S. EPA's mission is "to protect human health and the environment." The draft strategic plan for EPA outlines five goals including "Protect, sustain, or restore the health of people, communities, and ecosytems using integrated approaches and partnerships."

U.S. Fish and Wildlife Service (U.S.FWS)

http://www.fws.gov/

The U.S.FWS's mission is: "Working with others, to conserve, protect, and enhance fish, wildlife, and their habitats for the continuing benefit of the American people." The U.S.FWS has adopted an ecosystem management approach organized by U.S.GS ecosystem units and U.S.GS-defined watersheds.

National Biological Information Infrastructure

http://www.nbii.gov/geographic/us/federal.html

The National Biological Information Infrastructure(NBII) was established in the U.S. Geological Survey in 1998 as a broad, collaborative program to provide increased access to data and information on biological resources in the United States. The NBII is composed of a network of ten nodes (regional, thematic, infrastructure) which serve as "entry points" to provide: geospatial information, software, protocols, and reference data.

U.S. Geological Survey, Biological Resources Discipline (BRD)

http://biology.usgs.gov/

The BRD mission is "to work with others to provide the scientific understanding and technologies needed to support the sound management and conservation of our Nation's biological resources. BRD manages a number of national activites including: Biomonitoring of Environmental Status and Trends (BEST); Bird Banding Laboratory (BBL); Gap Analysis Program (GAP); Global Change Research Program; Geospatial Technology Program; Integrated Taxonomic Information System (ITIS); Land Use History of North America (LUHNA); National Biological Information Infrastructure (NBII) (see above); National Water-Quality Assessment Program (NAWQA); North American Breeding Bird Survey; Nonindigenous Aquatic Species Program; National Park Flora and National Park Fauna databases; Science.gov; U.S. GS-National Park Service Vegetation Mapping Program

U.S. Geological Survey, Biological Resources Discipline, National Wetlands Information Center

http://www.nwrc.usgs.gov/

The mission of the National Wetlands Research Center is to develop and disseminate scientific information needed for understanding the ecology and values of our nation's wetlands and for managing and restoring wetland habitats and associated plant and animal communities. The center provides information on wetland habitats through a system of peer-reviewed journal articles, databases, synthesis reports, workshops, conferences, technical assistance, training, and information/library services. Center research includes a broad array of wetland projects, plus research on the ecology of a wide variety of plant and animal species and communities that are found in wetlands.

U.S.Department of Agriculture (USDA) Natural Resources Conservation Service (NRCS)

http://www.nrcs.usda.gov/

The Natural Resources Conservation Service provides leadership in a partnership effort to

Table 1.4. U.S. Biodiversity Organizations and Agencies.

Table 1.4., continued

help people conserve, maintain, and improve our natural resources and environment. NRCS assists local, state, and federal agencies, and private landowners with conservation expertise for soil, water, and other natural resources.

Non-Governmental Biodiversity Organizations

The Nature Conservancy (TNC)
http://nature.org/
TNC's mission is to: preserve the plants, animals and natural communities that represent the diversity of life on earth by protecting the lands and waters they need to survive. TNC works with communities, businesses, and individuals to protect valuable lands and waters worldwide.

The Sierra Club
http://www.sierraclub.org/
The Sierra Club's mission is to: Explore, enjoy, and protect the wild places of the earth; practice and promote the responsible use of the earth's ecosystems and resources; educate and enlist humanity to protect and restore the quality of the natural and human environment; and use all lawful means to carry out these objectives.

The World Resources Institute (WRI)
http://www.wri.org/
The WRI's mission is: "to move human society to live in ways that protect Earth's environment and its capacity to provide for the needs and aspirations of current and future generations. Because people are inspired by ideas, empowered by knowledge, and moved to change by greater understanding, WRI provides—and helps other institutions provide—objective information and practical proposals for policy and institutional change that will foster environmentally sound, socially equitable development."

Table 1.5. International Biodiversity Organizations and Conventions.

Increasing international awareness and concern for biodiversity has led to the establishment of many international conventions and organizations, including:

The Convention on Biological Diversity (CBD)
http://www.biodiv.org/
The Convention on Biological Diversity (CBD), part of the United Nations Environment Programme (UNEP), was established after the 1992 Earth Summit in Rio de Janeiro, in support of the comprehensive strategy for "sustainable development." The CBD establishes three main goals: the conservation of biological diversity, the sustainable use of its components, and the fair and equitable sharing of the benefits from the use of genetic resources. The agreement which currently has 168 countries signed covers all ecosystems, species, and genetic resources.

The Global Biodiversity Strategy
http://biodiv.wri.org/globalbiodiversitystrategy-pub-2550.html
The World Resources Institute (WRI), World Conservation Union (IUCN), and United Nations Environment Programme (UNEP), developed a global biodiversity strategy, published as: The Global Biodiversity Strategy: Guidelines for Action to Save, Study, and Use Earth's Biotic Wealth Sustainably and Equitably (1992). The strategy includes 85 specific proposals for action to conserve biodiversity at the national, international, and local levels.

It is intended to simulate fundamental changes in how individuals, nations, and organizations perceive, manage, and use the earth's biological wealth. The Strategy is a complement to the Convention on Biological Diversity (CBD) providing a framework for actions that should be taken by governments and non-governmental organizations in support of the Convention.

The World Conservation Union, (IUCN)
http://www.iucn.org
The World Conservation Union, founded in 1948, brings together nations, government agencies, and non-governmental organizations in a global partnership with more than 980 members in 140 countries. IUCN's mission is: "To influence, encourage and assist societies throughout the world to conserve the integrity and diversity of nature and to ensure that any use of natural resources is equitable and ecologically sustainable." IUCN's goals include: maintaining ecosystem integrity and addressing the massive loss in biodiversity through extinction crisis. IUCN's vision is for a just world that values and conserves nature. The Union has helped many countries to prepare National Conservation Strategies and demonstrates the application of its knowledge through the field projects it supervises.

The Convention on International Trade in Endangered Species of Wild Fauna and Flora (CITES)
http://www.cites.org/
The Convention on International Trade in Endangered Species of Wild Fauna and Flora (CITES) is an international agreement established to ensure that international trade in species and specimens of wild animals and plants does not threaten their survival. CITES was drafted in 1963 at a meeting of members of IUCN (The World Conservation Union), and became active in 1975. CITES is legally binding by providing a framework to be respected by each participating country, which has to adopt its own domestic legislation. CITES provides protection to more than 30,000 species of animals and plants, whether they are traded as live specimens, fur coats, or dried herbs.

The Convention on the Conservation of Migratory Species of Wild Animals (CMS)
http://www.cms.int
The Convention on the Conservation of Migratory Species of Wild Animals (also known as the Bonn Convention) aims to conserve terrestrial, marine, and avian migratory species. Countries that have signed the CMS work together to conserve migratory species and their habitats by providing strict protection for endangered migratory species, by concluding multilateral agreements for the conservation and management of migratory species, and by undertaking co-operative research activities. CMS has a focus on the conservation needs of 107 endangered migratory species—which are, on average, more at risk of becoming endangered than non-migratory species due to their requirements for multiple habitats and migration routes.

The Convention on Wetlands (Ramsar)
http://www.ramsar.org/
The Convention on Wetlands, signed in Ramsar, Iran, in 1971, is an intergovernmental treaty providing a framework for national action and international cooperation regarding the conservation and wise use of internationally-significant wetlands. The convention covers all aspects of wetland conservation and use. It recognizes wetlands as ecosystems that are extremely important for biodiversity conservation as well as for the well-being of human

Table 1.5. continued

communities. There are presently 136 contracting countries to the convention, with 1,250 RAMSAR wetland sites, totaling 106.9 million hectares in area.

The World Heritage Convention (UNESCO)
http://whc.unesco.org
The Convention Concerning the Protection of the World Cultural and Natural Heritage (the World Heritage Convention) was adopted by the General Conference of United Nations Educational, Scientific, and Cultural Organization in 1972. To date, more than 170 countries have joined the Convention. The primary mission of the World Heritage Convention is to identify and conserve the world's cultural and natural heritage, by drawing up a list of sites whose outstanding values should be preserved for all humanity and to ensure their protection through a closer co-operation among nations.

CHAPTER 2

WOODLAND PARK ZOO

Kiki
Beyond the open door
Shadows bend,

Whose eyes hear water
Near the tree who grew a stream
Birds appear and disappear

Whose water face makes friends
Whose eyes see clouds of wind in his hair
What's in that hole,
Deepness doesn't move?

Who are those beyond the leaves?
Take my hand.

A poem by Grant Jones about Kiki's first day in
the new gorilla exhibit at Woodland Park Zoo, in 1979.

Zoos play an important role in the conservation of biodiversity—not only as refuges or places for captive breeding but as centers for education, raising humans' intellectual understanding of the world environment and its species, and building an emotional attachment with species other than our own. When people see animals living in an accurate replication of their natural habitat and engaging in natural social behaviors, they begin to respect animals as having a dignified existence in their own right, and they may become more interested in protecting wild habitats. On the contrary, animals confined to concrete cages and separated from the public by metal bars garner little sympathy or understanding. As David Hancocks argues in *A Different Nature* (2001, 160), "zoos can and must become gateways to the wild, metaphorically and practically." Landscape architects can play an important role in the future development of zoos in the United States and worldwide by bringing together interdisciplinary teams and coordinating the science necessary to create successful, biocentric zoos (see Figure 2.1; see also Figure 2.2 in color insert).

Zoos have evolved significantly since the first public zoos were created two hundred years ago (Figure 2.3). Despite their current roles as conservation centers, however, many zoos still base their design on an anthropocentric, rather than a biocentric, point of view. The architecture and landscape architecture firm of Jones & Jones, located in Seattle, Washington, succeeded in making the fundamental change to a biocentric perspective at the Woodland Park Zoo in Seattle. Inventing the concept of

Figure 2.1. Lowland gorilla climbing a tree inside an exhibit at Woodland Park Zoo.

Source: Jones & Jones, Architects and Landscape Architects, Ltd.

landscape immersion, a term coined by Grant Jones, they became the first zoo designers to describe the animals as clients (Jones 1982).

PROJECT DATA

The Woodland Park Zoo long-range plan was completed in 1976 by Jones & Jones, Architects and Landscape Architects, Ltd. The ninety-acre (36.4-hectare) zoo is situated in the northwest sector of Seattle, Washington, and is bounded on the east by Aurora Avenue, on the west by Phinney Avenue, and on the north and south by residential communities (Figure 2.4). In 1968, $4.5 million was set aside by the Forward Thrust Bond Issue for specific zoo improvements, based on a comprehensive plan. Because no such plan existed, an advisory committee called the Mayor's Zoo Action Task Force was formed, and the long-range plan was developed as a response to objectives set forth in 1975. Once the long-range plan was completed and approved in 1976, the actual projects contained within the plan (i.e., individual exhibits) were completed in phases as funding became available. While much funding has come from Forward Thrust monies, philanthropic support has helped complete numerous other improvements.

Landscape immersion emphasizes that animals in zoos should be exhibited in their natural environment (or the closest facsimile possible), which should reach out into the observation area so that visitors also experience the environment by standing in it rather than just looking at it. Cultural resonance, another term coined by Grant Jones, moves beyond landscape immersion to include aspects of the interdependent relationship between humans and animals in their native environment. For example, the architecture, religion, and culture of Southeast Asia is intimately tied to people's experience with elephants. The multipurpose, interdisciplinary design framework used by the

Evolution of Zoos

CONSERVATION CENTRE
Environmental Resource Centre

Theme	Environmental
Subjects	Ecosystems
	Survival of the Species
Concerns	Holistic conservation
	Organizational networks
Exhibitry	Immersion exhibits

21st century

ZOOLOGICAL PARK
Living Museum

Theme	Ecological
Subjects	Habitats of animals
	Behavioral biology
Concerns	Cooperative species
	management
	Professional development
Exhibitry	Dioramas

20th century

MENAGERIE
Natural History Cabinet

Theme	Taxonomic
Subjects	Diversity of species
	Adaptions for life
Concerns	Species husbandry
	Species propagation
Exhibitry	Cages

19th century

Figure 2.3. Over the past two hundred years, the purpose of zoos has evolved dramatically, from museum-like centers of natural history to environmental resource centers.

Source: World Zoo Organization 1993.

Figure 2.4. Woodland Park Zoo is located in a residential area of Seattle, Washington.

Source: Jones & Jones Architects and Landscape Architects, Ltd.

Figure 2.5. The design framework for the development of the Woodland Park Zoo long-range plan illustrates the "centripetal process" designed by Jones & Jones. The process included the synthesis of the following steps: inventory, analysis, generation of alternatives, and concept selection.

Source: Jones & Jones, Architects and Landscape Architects, Ltd.

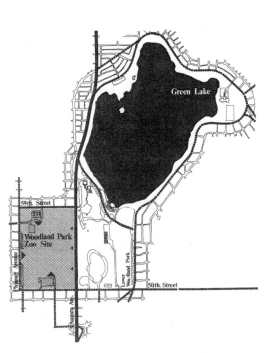

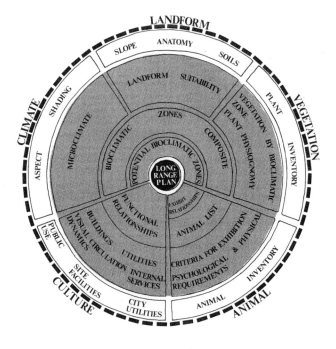

designers of Woodland Park Zoo is presented in Figure 2.5, which shows the particular influences on the long-range plan.

PROJECT PARTICIPANTS

The long-range plan was initiated by the City of Seattle in response to the requirements of the Forward Thrust Bond Issue in 1975 after a previous plan, developed by architect G. R. Bartholick, was rejected by a public initiative because of its monumental scale and incompatibility with the neighborhood. Many landscape architects and architects at Jones & Jones were closely involved in developing the master plan, including Grant R. Jones (the principal-in-charge), Jon Charles Coe, Johnpaul Jones, Peter Harvard, John Ady, David Walters, John Swanson, Eric Schmidt, and Keith Larson. Jim Brighton, a partner in the firm, noted that the landscape architects spent 95 percent of their project time acting as leaders and coordinators within interdisciplinary teams. Landscape architects are needed, he says, to pull together a conceptual idea and to give it a physical form. Jones & Jones was chosen for this project because they were known for their "groundbreaking methodology for reading a landscape to determine natural process and form" (Hancocks 2001, 113) as well as for their commitment to "placing nature first" in their designs. They further promoted this reputation with the Woodland Park Zoo long-range plan, which incorporated the concepts of landscape immersion and cultural resonance to fully engage visitors in the natural environments of the animals they came to observe (Jones & Jones 1976).

Consultants were also an integral part of the team, including Dennis Paulson, biologist; Donald Hogan, civil engineer; and Phillip Osborn, geologist. The interim director of the Woodland Park Zoo at the time was James Foster. The "living zoo" expert, David Hancocks, originally acted as design coordinator, establishing the presentation and exhibit themes, and later became the new zoo director. Trained as an architect, Hancocks had previously consulted with Ian McHarg on the Pardisan project in Iran (discussed below). Hancocks, who came to the Woodland Zoo project by retaining the services of Jones & Jones, sought to understand the landscape in order to determine the feasibility of organizing the zoo around the bioclimatology of plants. Dennis Paulson described the effort as "teamwork across disciplines," with no predefined roles. Additionally, members of the Forward Thrust Development Committee, the Seattle Design Commission, and many scholars and naturalists provided their input as the plan was developed. Community/public participation took the form of the Forward Thrust Development Committee, which acted as "the medium for accountability and continuity of intent" (Jones & Jones 1976, 1).

PROJECT GOALS AND OBJECTIVES

The stated goal of this project was set forth by the Zoo Action Task Force: "The Woodland Park Zoological Garden should be a Life Science Institute demonstrating the value and beauty as well as behavioral and physical adaptations of animal life. As such, primary emphasis should be placed on fostering public understanding of animal life and its relationship to ecological systems" (Jones & Jones 1976, 1).

As the long-range plan describes, a zoo differs from a natural history museum because it houses living animals; as such, it becomes "essential to give the animals all the necessary opportunities to engage in natural behavior, to the benefit of the animal and the zoo visitor" (Jones & Jones 1976, 4). To achieve this end, David Hancocks developed the exhibit theme of social biology by selecting larger, natural group sizes of fewer animal species, such as a band of gorillas (Figure 2.6 and Figure 2.7 in color insert) or a herd of antelope. This focus allows visitors to observe many different aspects of the animals, not just their morphological characteristics, and is intended to encourage people to reflect on their own social species. Another intention of the zoo was to provide visitors with a "total environmental experience." To this end, the presentation theme of bioclimatic zones moves away from conventional zoo design in that it presents the animals within microclimates that replicate natural climates, rather than dividing the zoo into different continents or zoogeographic areas (Jones & Jones 1976).

Like Woodland Park, Pardisan was designed at the same time by Wallace McHarg Roberts and Todd (WMRT) to provide an ecologically-based zoo environment and visitor experience on 1000 acres (400 hectares) in the Iranian desert in metropolitan Tehran (Figure 2.8 in color insert). The name Pardisan derives from the old Persian word *pardis*, which means a royal garden where "all good things the earth provides" might be enjoyed, and from which the English word paradise was derived (Mandala Collaborative/Wallace McHarg Roberts Todd 1975). WMRT planned an innovative zoo at Pardisan, unprecedented in scale and species diversity, where comparative examples of adaptation to specific regions of the world were analyzed to discern environmental analogues to those found in Iran (Figures 2.9 and 2.10) (McHarg 1996, 294). Jones & Jones worked with WMRT on the zoo design and contributed to species lists and exhibit scenarios, and the Pardisan work informed the Jones & Jones approach for Woodland

Figure 2.9. Animal and plant adaptations to the plateau desert of Iran.

Figure 2.10. Cisterns as human adaptations to the plateau desert of Iran.

Source for both: Mandala Collaborative/ Wallace McHarg Roberts Todd 1975; illustrations by Colin Franklin.

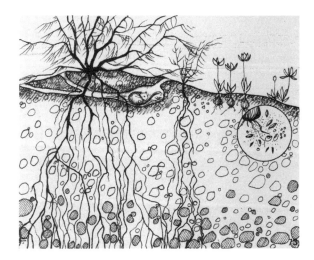

Park Zoo. Unfortunately, the visionary Pardisan project was never constructed due to radical social and political changes resulting from the Iranian Revolution.

The approach by Jones & Jones for Woodland Park Zoo marked a progressive departure from the status quo in zoo design, in which animals are displayed in habitats that fail to resemble their natural environment or, even worse, displayed in concrete cages with metal bars separating them from zoo visitors. Often, social animals are exhibited in solitary confinement, which leads to unnatural behaviors. In these situations, the animals not only are stripped of their dignity but often lose the chance of gaining sympathy from zoo visitors, who may see the animals negatively—for example, describing them as dirty or aggressive (Figure 2.11 in color insert). Additionally, most zoos advance a false image of animals, presenting a disproportionately large number of mammalian species and exotic species. In contrast, Woodland Park Zoo includes animals of regional importance, educating visitors about the biotic world immediately surrounding them as well as about environments far from the Pacific Northwest (Hancocks 2001).

Zoos have several main purposes: recreation, education, research, and conservation (Jones 1982). In 1993, the World Zoo Organization published the World Zoo Conservation Strategy, which notes that the greatest purpose of zoos and aquariums is to contribute to the conservation movement, whether directly (through captive breeding) or indirectly (through visitor awareness). Furthermore, as noted above, a greater emphasis on local or regional species is needed, as poor land use practices destroy more and more local habitat across the country. Grant Jones says that the true contribution (and justification) of zoos is the way they increase public awareness and concern for environmental issues. Likewise, Hancocks writes: "There is a very different need for zoos today and going to a zoo to see pandas and tigers is no longer sufficient justification for its existence" (2001, 160).

The priority at Woodland Park Zoo is clearly animal comfort and protection as well as increasing visitors' empathy for the animals they see and their wild cousins. Landscape immersion can reinforce emotional and cognitive learning (Berlein 2002). Grant Jones explained how Jones & Jones attempted to re-create the feelings people have when they're in the wilderness: feelings of being the intruder, of being very small in a big world. Woodland Park Zoo was designed to give visitors the perspective of being a guest "in the animal's domain" and of observing animals that behave and interact on their own terms.

PUBLIC/PRIVATE PARTNERSHIP AND COLLABORATION

Although members of the public were part of the Forward Thrust Development Committee, this project was mostly an institutional venture and did not involve citizens in the development of the long-range plan. Today, however, citizens are involved in reviewing the long-range plan as well as in fund-raising efforts for the zoo (Berlein 2002).

BIODIVERSITY DATA ISSUES AND
PLANNING STRATEGIES

Zoos can protect and conserve biodiversity in a number of ways. Directly, they can engage in captive breeding programs by participating in breeding networks with other zoos or in artificial breeding/cryopreservation efforts, though these efforts zoos play a limited role in protecting the survival of species. In this way, zoos can act as genetic reservoirs. The World Zoo Organization says that animals should only be removed from the wild if this action would benefit the long-term survival of the species; for this reason, giving space to endangered species and participating in breeding networks are vitally important activities.

Zoos can also conserve biodiversity indirectly, by educating visitors and encouraging future environmental action, such as contributing to an organization that protects a particular habitat or ecosystem. This is best accomplished when the zoo design evokes feelings of empathy among visitors. As David Hancocks describes in *A Different Nature*, people surveyed after visiting a conventional zoo where animals are kept behind bars had only negative comments to make about the animals, describing them as dirty and aggressive. People surveyed after visiting a zoo based on landscape immersion, however, described the animals as beautiful, strong, and interesting. These latter individuals also said they were more likely to contribute to an environmental cause after visiting the zoo. Grant Jones (1982) notes that it is crucial that zoo designers do not alienate the public by making them feel as if an animal would be better off extinct than in captivity. His article, in the American Association of Zoological Parks and Aquariums 1982 annual conference proceedings, provides a list of sixteen key "do's and don'ts" for designing a successful biocentric zoo (Table 2.1).

As mentioned above, the exhibition theme at the Woodland Park Zoo is social biology. To adhere to this theme, the zoo attempts to display natural-sized groups of social animals. Perhaps this results in fewer species than one might see in a conventional zoo, but also in a greater number of individuals within the species chosen so that they may interact with one another as they do in the wild (Jones & Jones 1976). Dennis Paulson, the project's consulting biologist, noted that the zoo concept was to show a "wonderful slice" of biodiversity, from megafauna to small mammals and birds (Paulson 2002). Also unlike conventional zoos, Woodland Park does not merely focus on charismatic megafauna, nor does it forget about the plants that contribute to the animals' habitat. In fact, choosing the vegetation that best replicates the climatic zones occurred before the selection of animal species for the exhibits.

The bioclimatic concept, which forms the basis for the exhibits, is itself based on the idea that "animals are generally confined within certain parts of the world by the cause-and-effect relations of climate and vegetation" (Jones & Jones 1976, 8). These habitats occur within different parts of the world and often on more than one continent. The habitat zones are classified as a function of three interacting, interdependent factors: temperature, precipitation, and evapotranspiration (Figure 2.12). Any habitat in the world can be classified based on these three parameters and can be characterized

Table 2.1. Do's and Don'ts of Zoo Design. Suggestions for design for a biocentric zoo by Grant Jones: adapted from the American Association of Zoological Parks and Aquariums annual conference proceedings, 1982.

- Viewers should not look down on the animals. Instead, animals should be at or above eye level.
- Animals should not be surrounded by viewers, because this does not allow "the dignity apparent when encountered in the wild." Instead, provide small overlooks that are screened from one another.
- Keep the animals only as close as their natural flight distances allows. Provide "alternative locations" within the exhibit so animals may chose where they want to be.
- Do not keep social animals in solitary confinement or in too small groups. In natural-sized groups, natural behaviors will be evident.
- Do not display disfigured or deformed animals, but do provide them with good, off-exhibit facilities.
- Do not display animals with human artifacts, which promotes anthropocentric attitudes.
- Do not allow props to "steal the show." Instead, reproduce natural habitat as faithfully as possible, without exaggeration or distortion.
- Use visible barriers only when absolutely necessary. Make it impossible to tell what contains the animals.
- Do not allow human cross viewing. Again, keep overlooks screened from one another. ("Nothing attracts human attention more than other humans.")
- Put viewing areas on secondary paths so that primary paths are not distracting to either people or animals.
- Do not allow an entire exhibit to be seen from one overlook.
- The exhibits should replicate the animal's natural environment.
- Do not put humans in man-made settings and animals in natural settings. Instead, immerse the viewer by extending the natural setting into human-use areas.
- Do not display animals from different habitats together in one natural habitat setting.
- Do not display animals from strikingly different habitats in adjacent spaces. Instead, relate them in habitat complexes that form transitional/ecotonal zones.
- Plan all elements of exhibits concurrently to create an integrated whole.

by a certain kind of vegetation expected in that life zone—for example, desert or temperate rain forest (Figure 2.13).

The bioclimatic zones at Woodland Park Zoo were determined primarily by using the Holdridge system, although Dennis Paulson also included some aspects of other systems before simplifying the procedure to apply it to the zoo. This approach is illustrated in Figure 2.14. Seattle, when placed on the Holdridge system triangle, can be found near the center, which allows a wide variety of plants to survive there (Jones & Jones 1976). By matching microclimates on site to global bioclimatic zones, the zoo designers were able to create exhibits that needed little or no modification, such as those found in temperate rain forest zones. This procedure also allowed the zoo to focus some attention on local habitats and species. Other exhibits needed only moderate modification (such as the inclusion of heat coils in rocks within the lowland gorilla

Figure 2.12. All world habitats, or bioclimatic zones, can be classified through the interaction of temperature, climate, and evapotranspiration.

Source: Jones & Jones, Architects and Landscape Architects, Ltd.

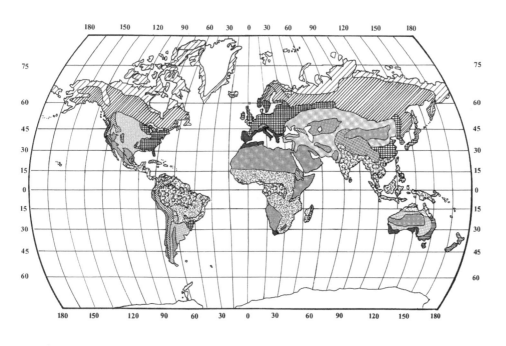

Figure 2.13. Map of world bioclimatic zones.

Source: Jones & Jones Architects and Landscape Architects, Ltd.

World Bioclimatic Zones

- Steppe
- Desert
- Chaparral
- Savanna
- Tundra
- Taiga
- Temperate Rain For.
- Temperate Deciduous For.
- Montane
- Tropical For.

Figure 2.14. The triangle illustrates the Holdridge System integrated with the bioclimatic zones chosen for replication at Woodland Park Zoo. Seattle is located in the center of the triangle, making it possible for many types of vegetation to survive with little or no modification of the natural landscape.

Source: Jones & Jones, Architects and Landscape Architects, Ltd.

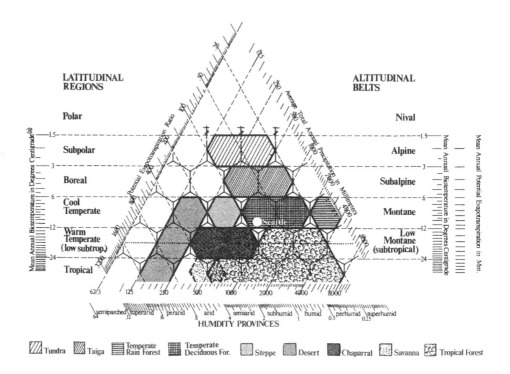

exhibit, or maximizing drainage to simulate desert habitats) to duplicate natural bioclimatic zones.

Once the bioclimatic zones were established and the associated vegetation chosen, animal species were selected. The ecologist's report for the zoo (Paulson n.d.) lists five attributes that should be considered when selecting animal species. These criteria are as follows (not in order of importance):

- Education—four factors of which are especially important: social behavior, evolutionary adaptations, convergent and parallel evolution, and adaptive radiation
- Interest—similar to education, and the rationale for exhibiting social species
- Representation—of diversity
- Research—some species, such as those with secretive habits, can be studied more effectively in a zoo environment
- Conservation—of species considered rare or endangered.

As discussed earlier, Jones & Jones based the design of Woodland Park Zoo on the idea of landscape immersion, described in the long-range plan (Jones & Jones 1976, 44) as follows:

Ideally, the viewer should move through the characteristic landscape of the bioclimatic zone, seeing its sights and savoring its moods. Only then can we become aware that the landscape is also inhabited by animals, separated by unseen barriers. The success of this landscape immersion depends entirely upon two factors:

1) the completeness with which the characteristic landscape is projected, and 2) the care and accuracy with which the viewpoints and views are located and composed, concealing barriers, enhancing perspectives, composing light and shadow, and, most importantly, visually unifying animal space and visual space.

In this way, no sense of separation between the animals and the visitors exists. Examples of specific ways to achieve concealed barriers and other aspects of landscape immersion are shown in Figure 2.17. This philosophy, expressed in physical form, is what truly moves Woodland Park Zoo away from conventional, anthropocentric design. Jon Charles Coe, a member of the Jones & Jones team, notes that immersion first appeals to the visitors' emotions and then to their intellect (Hancocks 2001). Careful attention to pedestrian circulation, the placement of recreation areas, and the bioclimatic sequence all contribute to the immersion effect. Zones are positioned within the zoo so that natural ecosystem transitions are evident, such as the placement of steppes exhibits next to deciduous forest and taiga exhibits. This attention to gradual transition further immerses visitors in the natural environments of the species displayed (Figure 2.15).

Conserving biodiversity in zoos seems to rely equally on which species are chosen as well as how those species are exhibited to the public. First and foremost, the comfort of the animals and their ability to engage in natural behavior must be achieved. Only then, through landscape immersion and the logical next step of cultural resonance, do visitors truly recognize animals as they exist in the wild, without bars (Figure 2.16). Cultural resonance is an idea that further shows visitors how animals and humans can and do (or did) survive side by side. Grant Jones describes this philosophy: "We believe that by combining the ideas of landscape immersion with those of cultural resonance, we have allowed the visitor to explore at the gut level, to reap the benefits of a feeling of interconnectedness . . . and to really sense our dependency on the planet for our humanness" (Jones 1989, 412).

One example of the use of cultural resonance is the Asian elephant exhibit at Woodland Park Zoo. Here, human artifacts that played a part in the relationship between the humans and the elephants are included in the exhibit, illustrating the reliance people in Thailand had on the native elephants. The exhibit winds its way through a wood-

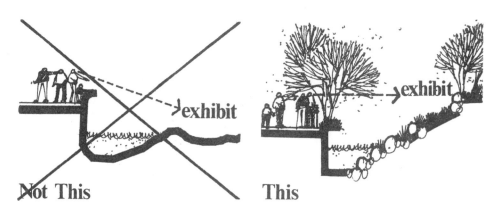

Figure 2.15. Two examples of exhibit guidelines described in the long-range plan for Woodland Park Zoo that illustrate the principles of landscape immersion.

Source: Jones & Jones, Architects and Landscape Architects, Ltd.

Tundra / Taiga   Montane / Temperate Rain Forest   Temp. Deciduous Forest / Steppe   Chaparral / Desert   Savanna / Tropical Forest   Water / Pedestrian & Vehicular Circulation

Long·Range Plan
Exhibit Development

JONES & JONES environmental planners · landscape architects · urban designers · architects
105 South Main Street Seattle, Washington 98104 (206) 624 5702

Inside Exhibit Enclosure
Outside Exhibit Enclos.
Passive Recreation
Inside Zoo Boundary
Outside Zoo Boundary

Bioclimatic Zone
Interpretive Center
Exhibit Interp. Center
Animal Service Area
Flight Cages & Aviaries

Meshed Exhibit
Wall
Fence
Ha-Ha
Zoo Boundary F.

Figure 2.16. The long-range plan for Woodland Park Zoo realized the potential of the site to support a wide range of global bioclimatic types that would support a diversity of animal exhibits in appropriate habitats.

Source: Jones & Jones, Architects and Landscape Architects, Ltd.

ed hillside, finally reaching the "Rong Chang," or the House of the Elephants. As the zoo's interpretive primer explains, the exhibit hopes to exhibit several "faces" of the elephants: "(1) elephants in the wild, (2) elephants as work animals in Thailand, and (3) elephants in Thai religious culture" (Jones 1989, 411). There is a simple lesson to be learned: if elephant habitat is lost, so are the elephants—and, consequently, the culture rooted in this landscape is gone, too. With this realization, zoo visitors can experience a deeper appreciation for the intrinsic role animals play in human existence. Landscape architects can contribute to this sympathetic education of visitors by designing exhibits sensitive to the ecological and cultural history of the ecosystem that is their focus.

POSTPROJECT EVALUATION

The Woodland Park Zoo Master Plan has been updated every four to five years. Most monitoring takes place on projects where risks were taken or where problems have

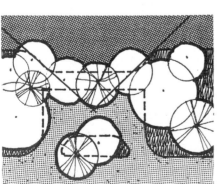

Figure 2.17. Jones & Jones designed eight viewing types to be used for all exhibits at the zoo. *Open edge* and *partially screened edge* types are shown on the left in plan and section views. *Mesh enclosure, shelter, animal day structure,* and *covered viewing into mesh enclosure* types are shown on the right. Note that no direct views are allowed from the busy primary paths.

Source: Jones & Jones, Architects and Landscape Architects, Ltd.

occurred—such as when an animal has escaped or when large amounts of vegetation have failed to thrive. Dennis Paulson explains that monitoring is the zoo's responsibility but that it usually isn't done. Grant Jones notes that zoo monitoring is often too simplistic and thus can reach the wrong conclusions. For example, if a tree dies in an exhibit, zoo staff may believe that it is best not to replace it. The correct response, however, might be to plant more trees in order to establish a microclimate more conducive to the tree's needs.

All participants interviewed said that it was important for zoos to be willing to take risks and to move beyond conservative, conventional design in order to truly be successful in providing quality habitat for the resident animals. Monitoring must address both animal and human responses. A zoo's success has conventionally been defined in terms of maintenance ease first, visitor appreciation second, and animal comfort third. In the new mind-set, however, this order would be reversed. Creating and maintaining exhibits that cater to the animals' needs and the immersion of viewers is not an easy task. It is, however, the only way that zoos will truly fulfill their obligations to the species they house.

Zoos present a new frontier for the protection of biodiversity, though their main role in this endeavor is often an indirect one. As David Hancocks (2001, 177) explains:

> It is time for zoos to reexamine their philosophies. People no longer need to visit a zoo to see what a camel or leopard looks like so much as to gain a better understanding of the dynamic systems of Nature and the interconnections within ecosystems, and most especially how to help conserve biological diversity on the planet. Zoos need to make the concept of biodiversity not just intelligible but wonderful to their audiences. It must be seen not just as fascinating, but as absolutely critical to the continuing health and well-being of people.

Landscape architects and planners can play an integral role in the future evolution of zoos as a unique application of biodiversity planning. Sensitive zoo design that successfully immerses viewers in the environment of the animals observed increases public awareness of a broad range of environmental issues, including biodiversity and habitat protection. Therefore, while the scale of a zoo site may be relatively small, it can have a far-reaching effect on biodiversity. It must be noted that many zoos have attempted landscape immersion techniques since Woodland Park Zoo was designed in 1976 (Clay 1980), and there is some danger in imitating only the process and not the underlying intent.

Landscape immersion is not simply naturalistic landscaping. Although, certainly, general principles exist that may be useful to all, zoo design should be specific to the site and to the animals that will live there. As Jones & Jones have said, the animal is the client, and this perspective can help the designer avoid conventional solutions. In this design application, as well as in many others, landscape architects play an important role as synthesizers of varied scientific and cultural information.

DEVENS FEDERAL MEDICAL CENTER COMPLEX: STORMWATER PROJECT

Planning for biodiversity requires coordinated preservation that employs defensive, offensive, and opportunistic strategies. A massive amount of upland and wetland habitat has been lost to urban development across the world. Some became disheartened by this loss and assumed a defensive posture and tried to stop all manner of change. Others, however, see the potential to re-create habitat opportunistically as part of the development process. The Devens, Massachusetts case is an example of the latter. It demonstrates how biodiversity improvement and wetland creation can be tagged on to development projects, to build public support, facilitate permitting, and produce net benefits for biodiversity as a result.

In the late 1980s, the U.S. government began closing major military bases nationwide, including Fort Devens in Ayer, Massachusetts. Like many other communities across the nation that faced base closings, local residents, merchants, and regional politicians feared economic hardship (White House 1999; Washington Transcript Service 1998). The federal government's plan for the reuse of the Devens site was diverse and promised 3,500 jobs for the area. The plan called for a combined federal prison and regional medical facility, an Army job training program, a business technology park, and programs for homeless relief. Portions of the post were designated for donation to the nearby Oxbow National Wildlife Refuge.

Initially, the process of redeveloping Fort Devens was fraught with obstacles. The U.S. Environmental Protection Agency (EPA) had listed the post as a Superfund site and began an investigation into fifty-four potential and known hazardous waste sites on the former Army post. Citing prior cases of difficult base closings, critics estimated the time frame for the transition process at twenty to thirty years. In addition, any plans had to navigate the difficult waters of town politics as the site straddled three communities, and special legislation and zoning changes required that plans be approved by all three adjacent communities, each of which held different views of what they wanted to see in the redeveloped Devens. According to an article in the December 9, 1994, *Boston Globe*, the working-class residents of Shirley and Ayer wanted job opportunities and no increased tax burden, while the more affluent residents of Harvard were more concerned about the environment.

An October 2, 1993, Associated Press story in the *Boston Globe* described how Congress had approved $74.6 million for a 240-acre (97.1-hectare) federal prison medical complex at the site, which was to be the first project launched on the former post. However, before any work could begin, the governor, the military, the surrounding communities, and the Federal Bureau of Prisons all had to approve the plan. The landscape architecture firm of Carol R. Johnson and Associates (CRJA) of Boston provided creative stormwater mitigation designs for the federal prison medical complex and was instrumental in leading the permitting process that set the tone for the redevelopment of the entire site.

PROJECT DATA

The site is located thirty-five miles west of Boston, Massachusetts, on the former Fort Devens Army post, adjacent to the towns of Ayer, Harvard, and Shirley. The Devens stormwater project was developed in the context of the permitting process and environmental impact report for a federal medical prison facility. CRJA were the project landscape architects responsible for designing the project in 1994–95, and they supervised project construction from 1995 to 1997 (Carol R. Johnson Associates 2002). The transformation of the Devens site became a new model for base redevelopment in which public concerns and desires were integrated with government plans.

CRJA began their work by assessing the natural history of the area. When examining historical photos, they found that a stream that ran through the site was fed by an underground spring and had once been much larger. Further research revealed that the Army's construction of a golf course had altered and culvertized the original stream corridor in the 1960s and reduced the flow significantly. Because of these modifications, the stream was deemed to have inadequate hydrologic capacity for stormwater flood control for the project. It had been channelized, was heavily silted, and received untreated surface discharge from both on- and off-site sources. CRJA aimed to transform the stream into a series of ponds that would not only provide greater flood storage capacity to accommodate estimated stormwater flows from the proposed construction but also to act like an undisturbed system would, filtering runoff and treating stormwater prior to discharging it into nearby Mirror Lake (Figure 3.1). In addition, the ponds were designed to provide breeding and feeding habitat for fish and other wildlife (Carol R. Johnson Ecological Services 1995).

After receiving approval, the project was constructed in phases. The first phase was to dechannelize the stream and relocate it to the north of the parking lot. During the next phase, the streambed was transformed into a connected pond system with three basins fed by runoff and a spring. The first basin was for sedimentation, the second was for filtration, and the third, which followed a gentle aeration cascade, was a deep, cold-water pool complete with a spawning shelf for fish and amphibians and a small island made by carefully excavating and grading around existing trees (Figures 3.2 and 3.3 in color insert) (Carol R. Johnson Associates 2002).

The system is designed to store stormwater during ten-year-peak storm periods with the aid of a weir and berm at the downstream edge of the third pond (Carol R. Johnson Ecological Services 1995; Carol R. Johnson Associates 2002). During construction, cocoa fiber mats and coir rolls planted with wetland vegetation from Bestmann Green Systems were placed along the banks of all three ponds (Figures 3.4 and 3.5 in color insert). This bioengineering prevented erosion during construction and helped establish permanent, native wetland vegetation and wildlife habitat along the waterway.

While the construction eliminated wetlands in the western portion of the site to allow for parking and buildings, the eastern part was excavated for stream relocation and pond construction. When the project was completed, it increased the total amount of surface water area by nearly fifteenfold, from 1,379 square feet to 20,104 square feet ($128m^2$, $1867m^2$) and added an additional 11,310 square feet ($1050m^2$), of vegetated wetland (Carol R. Johnson Ecological Services 1995). In addition, the landscape architects took great care to preserve as many mature trees on the site as possible by relocating or working around them (Figure 3.6 in color insert) (Carol R. Johnson Associates 2002). Clearly, the project produced a net gain in wetlands.

PROJECT PARTICIPANTS

The Federal Bureau of Prisons hired the architecture firm of Stubbins Associates of Boston to oversee the design and construction of a federal medical center complex for medium- and low-security inmates on the 300-acre (121.4-hectare) site consisting of wooded slopes, wetlands, streams, an Army hospital, and half of an ex-military golf course, all of which is located over a regional aquifer (Carol R. Johnson Ecological Services 1995).

The original Federal Bureau of Prisons plans showed buildings and parking areas spread throughout the site. This construction would have involved major grading of slopes, clearing woods, and filling wetlands. In an unusual move, Stubbins Associates appointed CRJA as the site team leaders and placed Bryant Associates Inc., the civil engineers on the project, under the direction of the landscape architects. In the lead role, CRJA proposed a bold alternative to confine buildings and parking to an already cleared and level 45-acre (18.2 hectare) plateau. The new design for the prison facility necessitated the clearing of only fifteen additional acres (six hectares) of land and the relocation of 1,400 square feet ($130m^2$) of a stream and part of its bordering vegetated wetland. This preserved the remaining 240 acres (97.1 hectares) of the site for open space, wetland, and woodland (Carol R. Johnson Ecological Services 1995). Working with representatives from the Federal Bureau of Prisons, Stubbins Associates, Bryant Associates, and Wendi Goldsmith (now of The Bioengineering Group), CRJA landscape architects and their senior ecologist Charlotte Cogswell assessed the site and worked to minimize impacts and improve the ecological functions of the site. They designed a water quality renovation system to improve groundwater recharge, flood control, and wildlife habitat while preserving existing forest and transforming the existing golf course into a natural meadow (Carol R. Johnson Associates 2002; Carol R. Johnson Ecological Services 1995).

CRJA landscape architects Randy Sorensen and John Amodeo were well versed in ecological aspects of the project and maintained clear communication with Cogswell throughout the process (Carol R. Johnson Associates 2000). CRJA not only worked to assess the site and design a solution but also collaborated with local governments and the Devens Enterprise Commission Regulatory Authority (DEC) to take their needs into consideration. Thus CRJA acted not only as designers but also as facilitators, as they steered the controversial project through the permitting process and helped the Federal Bureau of Prisons pioneer a progressive environmental solution, one that would serve as a model for redeveloping the entire area of Fort Devens.

PROJECT GOALS AND OBJECTIVES

From the beginning, CRJA viewed the Devens project as fulfilling multiple purposes. Its primary purpose was to treat and slow down stormwater from the built areas of the prison facility while providing overflow capacity for a one-hundred-year storm. However, CRJA also aimed to restore the historical stream corridor, provide more wildlife habitat both near and in the pond series, and create an aesthetically pleasing site for prison staff and visitors.

CRJA perceived the greater potential of this project because they understood the multiple issues and opportunities related to the small stream. They understood that federal defense base closings are typically controversial because they affect neighboring towns on many levels. They also realized that the area was already in the spotlight for environmental concerns because of its EPA Superfund listing, the presence of the nearby Oxbow National Wildlife Refuge and the Nashua River, the impacts of lighting pollution from the prison on bird migration routes, and the proximity of an underground aquifer.

Knowing that politicians, local governments, and the public wanted to see that a project has more benefits than liabilities, CRJA decided to add biodiversity enhancement to a list of improvements in order to gain support from a wider audience and to improve the prospects for fast-track permit approvals. Their proactive approach, coupling stormwater and wildlife benefits, was presented to local authorities as an improvement over existing conditions, which helped to ease the permitting process for the prison. Initially, the representatives at the Federal Bureau of Prisons were reluctant to adopt the more expensive design, but CRJA convinced them that the environmentally friendly approach would accelerate the permitting process while complying with new environmental regulations for federal projects mandating that work must go beyond compliance by being environmentally progressive (Carol R. Johnson Associates 2002).

Rather than becoming mired down in local controversy over the proposed prison, the project moved forward quickly, replacing the void left in the local economy by the closed military post. Arguably, the entire process was a win for all parties because the project boosted the local economy by creating high-quality jobs at the medical facility, improved the stormwater management at the site, provided more wildlife habitat than had previously existed, and served as a model for future redevelopment at Devens and beyond.

PUBLIC/PRIVATE PARTNERSHIP AND COLLABORATION

The Devens project represents a successful partnership between public and private interests; it was designed and constructed by private firms working for the Federal Bureau of Prisons. The project also required CRJA staff to collaborate with nearby towns and the DEC to understand and respond to local concerns. Surrounding towns were interested in the economic opportunities promised by the prison facility, but as stated above, many citizens were also concerned about environmental impacts. CRJA presented the project's environmental benefits to the public through a series of public workshops.

BIODIVERSITY DATA ISSUES AND PLANNING STRATEGIES

Original, site-specific biodiversity data were generated for the Devens project. A wildlife reconnaissance and assessment was conducted in May 1994 by Charlotte Cogswell and an ornithologist. They performed a field census of the types and quality of wildlife habitat at the site and looked for tracks, sounds, and other evidence of invertebrates, amphibians, mammals, and birds in the golf course stream, in nearby forested wetlands, and in the mixed hardwood/conifer forest. They found that amphibian breeding areas were limited along the stream due to channelization of the stream course. The stream also suffered from low flow and was nearly stagnant in some areas from silt and sediment deposited from crosswalk culverts (Carol R. Johnson Ecological Services 1995). The forested wetland and forest were observed to contain red-backed salamander (*Plethodon cinereus*), eastern chipmunk (*Tamias striatus*), raccoon (*Procyon lotor*), and several bird species. In the surrounding area, they found evidence of breeding habitat for many species, including but not limited to bullfrogs (*Rana catesbeiana*), Canada geese (*Branta canadensis*), killdeer (*Charadrius vociferus*), American robins (*Turdus migratorius*), red-winged blackbirds (*Agelaius phoeniceus*), and short-tailed shrews (*Blarina brevicouda*). The upland mixed hardwood and conifer forest offered habitat for red-tailed hawks (*Buteo jamaicensis*), hairy woodpeckers (*Picoides villosus*), warblers, jays, and other birds (Carol R. Johnson Ecological Services 1995).

A complete inventory of species found at the site is listed in Table 3.1. The assessment determined the limits of the bordering vegetative wetland that contained willow (*Salix spp.*), red maple (*Acer rubrum*), ash (*Fraxinus spp.*), and rush (*Jurnas spp.*). They also noted that the nearby Oxbow National Wildlife Refuge contains state-listed rare wetlands wildlife habitat as shown in the 1994 *Atlas of Estimated Habitats of State-listed Rare Wetlands Wildlife*, produced by the Massachusetts Natural Heritage and Endangered Species Program.

The Devens site was designed to restore the riparian function of the stream channel, improve stormwater management, and improve wildlife habitat. This tripartite

Table 3.1. Species List for Wildlife Found at the Devens Site during Carol R. Johnson and Associates' Wildlife Reconnaissance, May 20, 1994.

Source: Carol R. Johnson Ecological Services 1995.

strategy offered a proactive "restoration" scenario instead of a reactive "impact-mitigation" scenario (Carol R. Johnson Ecological Services 1995; Carol R. Johnson Associates 2002). The overall project is described as "an extensive wetland replication/restoration effort" (Carol R. Johnson Ecological Services 1995). CRJA did not target particular species with their design, nor did they consider such ecological principles as metapopulations or island biogeography theory. Rather, they adopted an anticipated habitat approach to planning for biodiversity, with the idea that "if you build it they will come." CRJA chose plants not only for their ability to stabilize banks but also for their ability to withstand periodic inundation caused by fluctuating water levels. (A complete inventory of plants used in the project is listed in Table 3.2.) Their aim was to build wetland habitat and restore the stream to a more healthy and undisturbed state, anticipating that this would generally benefit native species. In this way, the project team engaged in a proactive approach to biodiversity. The design used bioengineering to establish native wetland species, and it responded to the existing advantages of the site by preserving mature native trees.

BIRDS

Canada goose	*Branta canadensis*
mallard	*Anas platyrhynchos*
killdeer	*Charadrius vociferus*
mourning dove	*Zenaida macroura*
American crow	*Corvus brachyrhynchos*
black-capped chickadee	*Parus atricapillus*
American robin	*Turdus migratorius*
gray catbird	*Dumetella carolinensis*
European starling	*Sturnus vulgaris*
yellow warbler	*Dendroica petechia*
chipping sparrow	*Spizella passerina*
song sparrow	*Melospiza melodia*
red-winged blackbird	*Agelaius phoeniceus*
brown-headed cowbird	*Molothrus ater*
northern oriole	*Icterus galbula*
purple finch	*Carpodacus purpueus*
house finch	*Carpodacus mexicanus*
American goldfinch	*Carduelis tristis*
spotted sandpiper	*Actitis macularia*
eastern phoebe	*Sayornis phoebe*
tufted titmouse	*Parus bicolor*
veery	*Catharus fuscescens*
common yellowthroat	*Geothlyis trichas*
red-tailed hawk	*Buteo jamaicensis*
chimney swift	*Chaetura pelagica*
hairy woodpecker	*Picoides villosus*
northern flicker	*Colaptes auratus*
great crested flycatcher	*Myiarchus crinitus*
tree swallow	*Tachycineta bicolor*
bluejay	*Cyanocitta cristata*
white-breasted nuthatch	*Sitta carolinensis*
wood thrush	*Hylocichla mustelina*
northern parula	*Parula americana*
black-throated blue warbler	*Dendroica caerulescens*
blackburnian warbler	*Dendroica fusca*
yellow-rumped warbler	*Dendroica coronata*
pine warbler	*Dendroica pinus*
blackpoll warbler	*Dendroica striata*
scarlet tanager	*Piranga olivacea*

MAMMALS

eastern chipmunk	*Tamias striatus*
short-tailed shrew	*Biarina brevicouda*
woodchuck	*Marmota monax*
mouse	*Peramyscus*
vole	*Microtus* sp.
raccoon	*Procyon lotor*

AMPHIBIANS

bullfrog	*Rana catebeiana*
red-backed salamander	*Plethodon cinereus*

INVERTEBRATES

water snail	*Lymnaea palustris*
mosquito larvae	*Culicidae* sp.

POSTPROJECT EVALUATION

The project met the measurable objectives set out by CRJA: the permit was granted, the design was implemented, and the bioengineering aspects worked to prevent erosion and to jump-start the revegetation of the area with native species. The project is viewed as a model for future action by the DEC because CRJA helped the commission write its wetland protection regulations. The DEC serves as the wetland protection regulatory authority for the area and enforces the Massachusetts Wetlands Protection Act and the pursuant regulations (Devens Enterprise Commission Regulatory Authority 1999).

The Devens project has received attention from professionals who regard it as both a technical and an aesthetic success. It garnered an Environmental Achievement Award from the International Erosion Control Association for its combination of multiple

Table 3.2. Species list for plants used at the Devens site by Carol R. Johnson and Associates (CRJA Ecological Services 1995).

ice cutgrass	*Leersia oryziodes*	ebel tall fescue	*Festuca arundinacea*
fowl bluegrass	*Poa palustris*	palmer perennial ryegrass	*Lolium perenne*
rattlesnake mannagrass	*Glyceria canadensis*	Jamestown chewing fescue	*Festuca rubra* L. subsp.
fowl Manna grass	*Glyceria striata*		*Commutata*
blue flag	*Iris versicolor*		
cardinal flower	*Lobelia cardinalis*	Indian grass	*Sorghastrum nutans*
monkeyflower	*Mimulus ringens*	blackwell switchgrass	*Panicum virgatum*
sweetflag	*Acorus calamus*	little bluestem	*Schizachyrium scoparium*
tussock sedge	*Carex stricta*	blue joint reedgrass	*Calamagrostis canadensis*
shallow sedge	*Carex lurida*	alpine pussy toes	*Antennaria rosea*
fringed sedge	*Carex crinita*	purple coneflower	*Echinacea purpurea*
stalk-grain sedge	*Carex stipata*	ox-eye daisy	*Chrysanthemum*
Canadian rush	*Juncus canadensis*		*leucanthemum*
common rush	*Juncus effusus*	blackeyed Susan	*Rudbeckia hirta*
bluejoint reedgrass	*Calamagrostis canadensis*		
boneset herb	*Eupatorium perfolium*	inkberry	*Ilex glabra*
bulrush	*Scirpus rubrotinctus*	winterberry	*Ilex verticillata*
river bulrush	*Scirpus fluviatilis*	squashberry	*Viburnum edule*
narrow-leaf cattail	*Typha angustifolia*	spicebush	*Lindera benzoin*
bur-reed	*Sparaganium*	sweetpepperbush	*Clethra alnifolia*
American waterplantain	*Alisma plantago*	dwarf witchhalder	*Fothergilla gardenii*
arrow arum	*Peltandra virginica*	swamp azalea	*Rhododendron viscosum*
pickerelweed	*Pontedoria cordata*	mountain laurel	*Kalmia latifolia*
three-square reed	*Scirpus americanus*	gray birch	*Betula populifolia*
needle leaf arrowhead	*Saggitaria latifolia*	river birch	*Betula nigra*
		tupelo	*Nyssa sylvatica*
buttonbush	*Cephalanthus occidentalis*	red maple	*Acer rubrum*
silky dogwood	*Cornus amomum*	shadbush	*Amelanchier*
redosier dogwood	*Cornus stolinifera*	American larch	*Larix laricina*
goat willow	*Salix purpurea*	Canada hemlock	*Tsuga canadensis*
elderberry	*Sambucus canadensis*	white pine	*Pinus strobes*

features and multipurpose design goals (Goldsmith and Barret 1998; Barrent 1997), and it was featured in *Landscape Architecture* as an example of how detention ponds need not be "ugly single-purpose holes dug in the earth" (Thompson 1999, 44). Similarly, in the book *Sustainable Landscape Construction*, authors Thompson and Sorvig note that "this carefully engineered series of ponds looks as if it has always been there" (2000, 15).

The project ran into several roadblocks along the way. The government's Federal Appearances Memo dictated conservative limits on government spending intended solely for aesthetic purposes, forcing the elimination of native plantings close to the prison building; however, the bioengineering and herbaceous and woody wetland plantings within the vegetated wetland border that were associated with permits were retained. The project also tested everyone's faith in the design as significant water drawdown occurred during construction. Because of an unusually dry summer, the ponds filled slowly. For a brief period, it seemed as though CRJA had designed big, ugly holes in the earth (Carol R. Johnson Associates 2002).

The project presents some limits and drawbacks. No formal water quality testing has been done at the site, although changing the surrounding golf course into native meadows is expected to improve water quality by reducing contamination from turf fertilizers and chemicals. Field assessments of water quality entailed walk through and extrapolation by reading the site history (Carol R. Johnson Associates 2002). In addition, ecologist Charlotte Cogswell lamented the lack of monitoring. Because the client did not require monitoring, no funds were allocated for postconstruction analysis of the project. However, anecdotal evidence of wildlife at the site exists; prison staff has reported seeing red-tailed hawks (*Buteo jamaicensis*), red foxes (*Vulpes vulpes*), and other mammals near the ponds. Such lack of monitoring is a common problem for landscape restoration projects. Often, design projects allocate minimal funds for postconstruction activities at a site, and what funds do exist are usually usurped by maintenance costs. As for maintenance, CRJA,s design requires annual dredging of the sedimentation pond to prevent it from becoming a wet meadow and losing its aquatic habitat functionality (Carol R. Johnson Associates 2002).

The project missed a key opportunity to create stronger links with the Oxbow National Wildlife Refuge. It seems that CRJA was instructed by the Federal Bureau of Prisons to have no contact with parties except those involved in permitting; as a result, they did not have a chance to consult with the manager of the Oxbow National Wildlife Refuge, Tim Pryor. According to Pryor, although Mass Development (the authority responsible for overseeing the redevelopment of the post) did pass on some of the general stormwater basin plans, he never had any direct contact with anyone from CRJA (Pryor 2002). Pryor did not express concerns about the impacts that the project might have on the refuge, since none of the basins discharges directly into the refuge, but he could have been another source of biodiversity information if CRJA had looked more closely at landscape-scale connectivity opportunities for the habitat created at the site.

Judging from the relative speed of the permitting process and acceptance by the surrounding towns, the project has been well received by the public. A search of the media reveals no postconstruction criticism of the project, and indeed the conversion of the entire Devens site seems to have progressed smoothly. Today the Devens redevelopment area appears to be fulfilling its goal of providing economic opportunities for the region. As demonstrated by this project, landscape architects can lead clients through the process of developing sites in a more strategic way that simultaneously enhances site ecology and facilitates permitting processes, particularly in states with strict environmental regulations such as Massachusetts.

CROSSWINDS MARSH

Wetlands are well recognized as hotspots of biodiversity and providers of numerous hydrological, ecological, economic, and recreational functions (Table 4.1) (Pollack, Naiman, and Hanley 1998). Early environmental policy in the United States offered little protection and, in fact, enabled wetland drainage and filling on a widespread scale for agriculture and urban development. Of the 224 million acres (90.6 million hectares) of wetlands originally found in the lower forty-eight states, 53 percent has been lost (Dahl 2000). Although wetlands loss has declined in recent years, about 1.2 million acres (485,633 hectares) were lost in the United States from 1985 to 1995. The Clean Water Act's goal of achieving "no net loss" of wetlands in the United States has yet to be achieved. As noted by the Associated Press on September 17, 1997, the amount of wetlands continues to shrink even though 78,000 acres (31,566 hectares) are restored or mitigated annually in the United States (U.S. Fish and Wildlife Service 1997).

Wetland ecosystems are estimated to be second to tropical rain forests in the numbers of plant and animal species that depend on them for food and habitat (Environmental Defense and the Texas Center for Policy Studies 2003). Although they cover only 1 percent of the earth's surface, freshwater wetlands are believed to hold more than 40 percent of all species on earth, and 12 percent of animal species (RAMSAR 2003). The biodiversity found in wetlands sustains a valuable reservoir of genetic material that is vital to maintaining a sufficient level of variation as a buffer against diseases and pests in food crops. Additionally, wetlands, as important components of larger undisturbed ecosystems, have aesthetic values that can be quantified through revenues generated by ecotourism and by the amount that individuals and institutions are willing to pay for the conservation of species and ecosystems (Table 4.1).

Wetlands in populated and coastal areas are often isolated or surrounded by intensive land uses. The contemporary demand for space to support agriculture, urban development, and infrastructure routinely conflicts with and isolates these relict wetlands. In response to this inherent conflict of land use and space, wetland mitigation has become a common practice in most broad-scale land development projects (Zedler 1996). In most mitigation projects, new wetlands are "created" or restored to compensate for the

Table 4.1. Wetland functions. (Sipple 2002).

1. **Food Production**
   The combination of shallow water, high levels of inorganic nutrients, and high rates of primary productivity in many wetlands support organisms that form the base of the food web.

2. **Biogeochemical Cycling**
   Wetlands support biological, physical, and chemical transformations of various nutrients within the biota, soils, water, and air. Wetlands are particularly important in nitrogen, sulfur, and phosphorous cycling.

3. **Habitat for Fish, Wildlife, and Plants**
   Wetlands are primary habitats for many species. For other species, wetlands provide important seasonal or foraging habitats where food, water, and cover are plentiful.

4. **Improving Water Quality and Hydrology**
   Wetlands improve water quality by intercepting surface runoff and removing or retaining inorganic nutrients, processing organic wastes, and reducing suspended sediments before they reach open water.

5. **Flood Protection**
   Wetlands store and slowly release surface water, rain, snowmelt, groundwater, and floodwaters. Wetlands flood storage lowers flood peaks and reduces downstream erosion.

6. **Shoreline Erosion**
   Coastal wetlands protect shorelines and stream banks against erosion by stabilizing soil with roots, absorbing wave energy, and breaking up the flow of stream and river currents.

7. **Economic Benefits**
   Wetlands provide economically important products including mammals, birds, fish, shellfish, and timber.

8. **Recreational, Educational, and Research opportunities.**
   Wetlands provide significant opportunity for recreation, education, and research.

disturbance or destruction of an existing wetland. Wetlands are typically mitigated "in-kind" (for example, wet meadow to wet meadow) and in a location that is hydrologically linked or contiguous with the disturbed wetland. An area multiplier (i.e., 1.5 to 1.0) is often applied to acknowledge the difficulty of replicating all the functions of an existing wetland and the overall uncertainty of successfully reestablishing the complex ecology of wetlands. Although typically based on replicating the biophysical functions of wetlands, the mitigation multipliers usually fail to adequately consider the ecological services that wetlands provide, including flood protection, water quality improvement, and aesthetic enjoyment (Boyd and Wainger 2002).

Wetlands mitigation spans a full range of strategic planning responses (Ahern 1995). These include the following:

- Protective—setting aside and buffering healthy, well-functioning wetlands before they are isolated or threatened.
- Defensive—buffering or stabilizing wetlands under stress or pressure from adjacent land uses or from pending land use change.

- Offensive—creating or restoring "new" wetlands to compensate for wetlands lost previously in the local environment or elsewhere.
- Opportunistic—realizing multiple or collateral benefits through wetlands mitigation and taking advantage of special opportunities associated with development (e.g., stormwater management, recreation, or environmental education).

Conservation planning generally follows a protective strategy that focuses on hotspots of biodiversity. In most development projects, defensive or offensive strategies are applied to minimize impact on wetlands and to restore wetland functions, including biodiversity (Arendt 1999; Lecesse 1996).

Landscape architects and planners are regularly involved with all phases of wetland mitigation projects, including wetland delineation, project planning and design, mitigation planning and permitting, construction supervision, and postconstruction monitoring. The field of ecological restoration holds great potential for landscape architects but may require new pedagogical approaches, including significant and credible field experience (Owens-Viani 2002).

Mitigation projects challenge practitioners to realize multiple functions that may not have existed previously or to integrate mitigated wetlands into a broader, multipurpose landscape project. If project planning and design can move toward an integrated response that combines multiple strategies, great opportunities exist to restore ecological and hydrological functions and to add value and meaning for human use and education. Crosswinds Marsh is a project that demonstrates the potential of opportunistic, multi-objective wetlands mitigation for biodiversity restoration. It also demonstrates the particular roles that landscape architects can play in such projects and how they can add value at multiple points in the process.

PROJECT DATA

Crosswinds Marsh is a 1,400-acre (566 hectare) multipurpose wetland mitigation project located in southwestern Wayne County, Michigan. The project originated in 1986 when the Detroit Metropolitan Wayne County Airport updated its master plan, including a major runway expansion requiring extensive wetlands disturbance and mitigation. The scale of the mitigation and space limitations at the airport site led airport managers to seek an "off-airport" mitigation site within the same watershed. SmithGroup JJR (then known as Johnson Johnson & Roy Inc.) served as the prime consultant for the project (Dennison 2000). A location in Sumpter Township was selected for the mitigation site because it was sufficiently large, was located in a rural portion of Wayne County, and had the hydrological "potential" to support the required area needed for mitigation (Figure 4.1).

The property acquired from private landowners by Wayne County in Sumpter Township exceeds 1,400 acres (567 hectares); of this total, about 620 acres (250 hectares) of wetlands have been created or restored at Crosswinds Marsh. In phase 1, approximately 320 acres (130 hectares) of new wetlands were designed by SmithGroup JJR. Phase two, the final phase, was completed in 2000. All work was managed by the Wayne County Department of Airports (Hypner 2001). During the 1990s, the project proceeded through planning, permitting, construction, establishment, and monitoring. As the project was implemented, it grew well beyond a wetland mitigation project, adding significant biodiversity and public use components (Dennison 2000; Ott 2001). It has since become an award-winning project, receiving the President's Award of Excellence from the American Society of Landscape Architects in 1999 (Martin 2000). Crosswinds Marsh is now a successful Wayne County Park and Environmental Education Center. New data from monitoring has produced new knowledge for wetland restoration elsewhere in Michigan and throughout the midwestern United States.

Crosswinds Marsh is located in an area of low relief formed on ancient Lake Erie lakebed sediments, including beach ridges and a hydrological pattern composed of several meandering channels. Historically, the site supported a wet prairie, marshlands, and a wooded wetland landscape, which had been artificially drained with agricultural ditches and tile drains to support row crops (corn and soybeans), pasture, and hayfields. At the project's beginning in the early 1990s, a large proportion of the site was still used for agriculture. The remainder was in residential use or in the process of woodland succession.

Project mitigation goals were developed through consultation among the U.S. Environmental Protection Agency (EPA), the U.S. Fish and Wildlife Service (USFWS), the Michigan Department of Natural Resources (now the Michigan Department of Environmental Quality and referred to in the remainder of this chapter as MDEQ), various Wayne County departments, a citizen's advisory committee, and SmithGroup JJR. The resulting goals included a range of wetland types: forested, wet meadow, emergent, shallow open water, and deep water. The first three types were required as compensation for impacts to forested, wet meadow, and emergent wetlands at the airport. The deep-water wetland was added to establish a warm-water fishery (Dennison 2001).

MDEQ was responsible for reviewing and approving the permit, which required a 1.5:1 mitigation ratio for the 311 acres (125 hectares) of wetlands that were to be disturbed for the runway expansion and associated projects at the Detroit Metropolitan Wayne County Airport. The Crosswinds site was proposed in response to consultations with the permitting agencies (principally the MDEQ, EPA, and USFWS). At the time, several conclusions were reached regarding the location of the mitigation site. First, an off-airport site would avoid unnecessary hazards to aircraft from waterfowl. Second, an out-of-basin location was required to provide sufficient undeveloped land and to minimize community impacts. Finally, a larger site was considered preferable to several smaller sites for creating more valuable wildlife habitat (Ott 2001).

At the time it was constructed, Crosswinds Marsh was the largest single mitigation project in the United States. The project consisted of a massive earth-moving effort involving more than 750,000 cubic yards (573,450 cubic meters) of earth to create a wetland basin ranging from 0 to 20 feet (0 to 6 meters) deep (Figure 4.2). The total cost of the Crosswinds Marsh project approximated $12 million, 75 percent of which was paid with federal runway expansion funds from the Federal Aviation Administration. The project began with strong support from the airport and from Wayne County to enable the airport expansion. Its large scale garnered public attention and interest in providing additional functions and benefits to the project, including biodiversity, public access, and recreation. SmithGroup JJR worked with all parties to integrate these objectives and functions within the mitigation project (Dennison 2000).

PROJECT PARTICIPANTS

Crosswinds Marsh involved a large complement of federal, state, and county agencies. The Federal Aviation Administration provided funding through airport bonds (Hypner 2001). MDEQ was responsible for reviewing and approving all permits. Wayne County department supervisors, staff at Detroit Metropolitan Wayne County Airport, and Sumpter Township officials were involved in the overall review and permitting of the project.

SmithGroup JJR was the prime consultant for planning, design, and engineering. The project was managed within the SmithGroup JJR Environmental Studio, which includes landscape architects and environmental scientists working in an interdisciplinary setting. The professionals involved included Gary Crawford and Catherine Riseng (aquatic macro-invertebrates, fish and water quality) and William Brodowicz (plants). Subconsultants included Allen Kurta (Eastern Michigan University; reptiles, amphibians, mammals) and Stephen Hinshaw (University of Michigan; birds). The scientists conducted baseline data collection and post-implementation monitoring, while the landscape architects made the design decisions, produced the working drawings, and supervised project construction (Dennison 2001; Ott 2001).

The SmithGroup JJR project team collaborated to establish an "ecological framework" for the project regarding how much mitigation flexibility was possible. The landscape architects' initial role was to provide an understanding of the presettlement vegetation context and to interpret and apply rigorous science to the project. Throughout the project, landscape architects led the interdisciplinary team, researching habitat design methods and experimenting with alternative soil mediums and planting methods (e.g. no topsoil, sand, planting in raised furrows, using different size plants). The landscape architects also led the planning of the public use component of the project, including boardwalks and hiking, equestrian, and canoe trails (Figure 4.3). They also successfully advocated for the inclusion of boardwalks, trails, and an arrival-educational wetland center (Figures 4.4 and 4.5).

Project engineers were involved with the hydrologic modeling to address any concerns for postmitigation flooding of areas adjacent to the Crosswinds Marsh site. Two drainage channels existed at the site, the Disbrow and the Clark-Morey. The project engineers determined that the Disbrow Drain could continue to flow into and through the marsh to serve as the wetland's primary hydrological source and to improve downstream water quality. The Clark-Morey Drain, which had impaired water quality, was diverted around the perimeter of the marsh to maintain hydrological isolation. The engineers also recommended the use of clay cut-off walls to hydrologically isolate the marsh from its surroundings, which include a regional landfill situated down gradient. The engineers designed and set the concrete outflow control structure to establish the base water elevation for the entire project. The control structure reinforced the earlier decision to stop upstream fish migration because of concerns about immigration of undesirable fish species, including common carp (*Cyprinus carpio*) and gizard shad (*Dorosoma cepedianum*).

Several groups participated as part of the citizen's advisory committee; among the more active participants were the Michigan United Conservation Club, the East Michigan Environmental Action Council, and the University of Michigan, Dearborn. Their interest focused on the type and location of public use appropriate for the site in the context of wetland mitigation—the primary goal—and associated habitat creation.

PROJECT GOALS AND OBJECTIVES

The Crosswinds Marsh project began solely as a compensatory wetlands mitigation project. Thus the principal goal was to satisfy the requirements of the MDEQ permit to enable the runway expansion to be built. The permit specifically required that the mitigation be "sufficient in terms of physical characteristics, water supply, and any other pertinent ecological factors to create the desired wetland types" (Michigan Department of Natural Resources 1991).

As the project evolved, SmithGroup JJR, working in collaboration with Wayne County, advocated three additional goals for the project:
1. To develop educational and passive recreational use
2. To provide opportunity for public use
3. To establish Crosswinds Marsh as a county-sponsored "Wetland Interpretive Reserve"

According to the mitigation plan, these additional goals were added to provide "a variety of environmental and social functions in perpetuity" (Johnson Johnson & Roy/Inc. 1991). It was also important to the county to address local concerns that arose from the displacement of about thirty individuals from their homes and the loss of nearly 1,400 acres (567 hectares) of land from the township tax base, which had previously been under private ownership.

PUBLIC/PRIVATE PARTNERSHIP AND COLLABORATION

The process of project permitting, design, and implementation involved multiple public and private organizations and interests. The local community was involved as various project concepts were developed. Initially, the community did not understand or appreciate the potential benefits of such a large-scale mitigation project. The plan was understood simply as a "big swamp"—displacing farmland and local residents while offering little or no positive attributes (Bauer 2001). Several community hearings were held to raise public awareness and understanding of the project's requirements and its potential to become a significant asset for the county.

The Michigan United Conservation Clubs were involved during the evolution of the project along with the other members of the township and the county. Sumpter Township asked for hunting access to the wetland, but this was denied for safety concern reasons. As a direct result of the public hearings, and of the project's successful implementation, Crosswinds Marsh evolved in the community's eyes from a swamp into a successful county park for use by local residents. Perimeter upland trails were installed for equestrians, and an extensive system of drains, trails (accessible per the standards set forth in the Americans with Disabilities Act), and boardwalks were located throughout the site (Figures 4.6 and 4.7).

BIODIVERSITY DATA ISSUES AND PLANNING STRATEGIES

As in most mitigation and restoration projects, Crosswinds Marsh confronted a distinct lack of data regarding the specific ecosystems, plant communities, and biota involved. To overcome this lack of information, the project planners and designers conducted two complementary lines of research: a review of published literature and an inventory of adjacent and reference wetlands. SmithGroup JJR researched vegetation by examining the only available source of this site-specific information: presettlement mapping and historical survey maps. An inventory was made of existing wetlands habitats in Wayne County to identify the diversity and distribution of plants and animals surrounding the project area. This inventory influenced the development mitigation plan by producing species lists and associating wetlands habitats with particular wetland species.

Botanical surveys at the mitigation site found no threatened or endangered wildlife species. However, threatened and endangered flora species were found at the airport; these species were documented and protected with fencing to avoid disturbing them during runway construction. Selected occurrences of at-risk endangered plant species were relocated with a tree spade to a suitable location within the mitigation site. The design of suitable habitat for the plant species was based largely on identifying soil types and hydrological conditions comparable to those present at the airport. The soils were identified after a thorough review of existing conditions at the mitigation site, while appropriate hydrological conditions were established by using monitoring wells at both the airport and the mitigation area and then grading the mitigation site to achieve comparable hydrological conditions.

The Disbrow Drain supported a warm-water fishery and macro-invertebrate population typically found in agricultural drains, freshwater marshes, and shallow water communities. Results of the initial aquatic surveys, however, indicated that large numbers of common carp (*Cyprinus carpio*) and gizard shad (*Dorosoma cepledignum*) migrating from Lake Erie were disrupting in-stream habitat, dislodging macro-invertebrates, and displacing resident fish. This prompted the decision to "isolate" the hydrologic regime of the wetlands by cutting off upstream migration potential from the Disbrow Drain.

The literature review, site investigations, and survey of nearby reference wetlands provided sufficient information to produce a comprehensive mitigation plan. The plan was developed in phases initially determined by the grading plan, which established a diversity of water depths correlated with specific wetland types. The planting plan applied a range of management establishment techniques to restore diversity or wetland and upland habitats (Table 4.2)

POSTPROJECT EVALUATION

The Floristic Quality Assessment system was used in the monitoring process at the site (Herman et al. 1996). Continual monitoring of twenty transects over five years has not only documented the establishment rates for mitigation species but showed how the proportion of species has changed in response to seasonal moisture conditions. A minimum of two transects was established in each habitat type (two total of eleven transects), with 10.8-square-foot (1 square meter) plots established every 50 feet (16

Table 4.2. Relationship of management/establishment techniques with target plant communities. (Smith Group JJR).

Wetland Type	Area (acres/hectares)	Percent	Proposed Hydrologic Regime	Revegetation Technique
Forested wetland/scrub shrub	335.6 ac/136 ha	54	Seasonally flooded	Bare root stock, tree seeds, seedlings
Wet meadow	120 ac/48.6 ha	19	Saturated	Seeding of grasses and forbs
Emergent wetland	102 ac/41.3 ha	16	0–2 feet 0–0.6 meters	Seeding and tubers
Shallow water wetland	29 ac/11.7 ha	5	2–3 feet 0.6–0.91 meters	Tubers and root stock
Deep water wetland	27 ac/10.9 ha	5	3–6.5 feet 0.91–2 meters	Tubers and root stock
Deepwater aquatic habitat	6 ac/2.4 ha	1	6.5–12 feet 2–3.6 meters	Submerged tree masses
Total wetland mitigation area	620 ac/251 ha	100		

Note: Depth greater than 2 meters not credited as compensatory mitigation. Quantities identified above represent in-kind replacement at a ratio of 1.5 to 1.0.

meters) along the transect. The center of each plot was marked with stakes. Plots were selected to represent planted and unplanted areas. Permit-required wetland monitoring was conducted from 1994 to 1998. Additional monitoring of a subset of plots took place on the county's own initiative in 1999. In addition to photographs, the information recorded for each plot included percentage cover, frequency of indicator species, water level, and pH (Dennison 2001; Johnson Johnson & Roy 1999).

Hydrology was monitored twice a year in spring and late summer, recording readings from water-depth gauges and groundwater wells. Water quality was monitored three times a year, in late spring, summer, and fall, at permanent entering and exiting sample points. Temperature, dissolved oxygen, pH, and conductivity were also measured. The hydrologic and water quality data collection has been discontinued. Wayne County does continue to collect water-quality data for bacteria because canoe rentals involve water contact.

Several classes of fauna were monitored: birds, herptiles, and mammals. Birds were monitored three times each year, during the spring migration and in summer and fall. Specific stations were visited in the morning for a five-minute observation that included visual and audio observations as well as callbacks (human-initiated birdcalls). The herptiles were monitored in conjunction with the vegetation sampling three times each year. Amphibians and reptiles were also monitored from March to June using night trapping, with drift fences and pitfall traps. Mammals were monitored with live traps set along the permanent transects. Muskrat houses and evidence of muskrat grazing were also noted.

Finally, aquatic biology was monitored three times a year in spring, summer, and fall using a stratified random sample. Macro-invertebrates were analyzed in July at seven locations for tolerance rating using the Shannon-Weaver diversity index (Shannon and Weaver 1949). Fisheries were monitored using seines in shallow water and gill nets in deeper water to note species type and size (Dennison 2001).

MDEQ required five years of monitoring overall and ten years of monitoring for the protected plant species moved from the airport to the site adjacent to Crosswinds Marsh. This requirement was not appreciated by the airport personnel who initially assumed that monitoring results could "trigger" additional mitigation work. The monitoring requirement also raised concern over project "closure" because it required a five- to ten-year wait after the project was otherwise complete. The monitoring requirement extended well beyond the project contractors' two-year guarantee period on planting. During the project, an "uneasy" relationship existed among Wayne County, the State of Michigan, and the several federal agencies involved. Concerns also arose about changing personnel in the regulatory agencies, and anxiety developed over the timing of the final project approval and sign-off.

Monitoring documented that several areas had been invaded by exotic species, including common reed (*Phragmites australis*) and loosestrife (*Lythrum salicaria*). These species were 75 to 80 percent eliminated through targeted treatments with the herbicide Rodeo. The sites were replanted and are now being monitored and controlled with nonchemical controls.

As the wetland vegetation was becoming established, large areas of clay exposed during construction caused high turbidity in the open-water area of the wetland. The long orientation of open water parallel to the prevailing westerly winds produced significant wind fetch, causing elevated rates of water movement and increased turbidity. In the early years, carp proliferated in the wetland, exacerbating the turbidity problem by continually stirring up the bottom clay during feeding. The turbidity has lessened as aquatic vegetation has become established, stabilizing the clay substrate. The predominant plants established in the open water include Eurasian water-milfoil (*Myriophyllum spicatum*), curly pondweed (*Potamogeton crispus*), and brittle waternymph (*Najas minor*). As the water quality has improved with project maturation, predatory fish species (such as bass) micropterus ssp., which feed on and limit the number of small carp (*Cyprinus carpio*), have become established.

To the surprise and delight of the project designers and the county park staff, bald eagles (*Haliaeetus leucocephalus*) have moved into a stand of trees adjacent to the wetland (Figure 4.7). The primary nest tree is located in a woodlot adjoining the main area of open water that was flooded by rising water levels. This location overlooks much of the open-water area at Crosswinds and is the last area to freeze in winter, ensuring a nearly constant feeding habitat for the eagles. The eagles presence gives the project high public visibility, lending credibility to Crosswinds as a bona fide "nature preserve" and wetland study center. Their appearance has influenced project management—for example, eliminating the possible use of rotenone to kill the carp species in the wetlands.

The issue of invasive species, as well as other aspects of the project, has taken on an educational component under Wayne County Parks staff management. Private boats are excluded because of the risk of importing zebra mussels (*Dreissena polymorpha*) to the wetland. Instead, rental canoes meet the recreational demand. Education programs thus discuss invasive species in the broader context of biodiversity.

Lessons learned at this site have been applied to the phase two mitigation project adjacent to Crosswinds Marsh, which was approved with certain modifications to the design based on the results of the phase one wetlands construction. This additional mitigation emphasized forested wetlands and restricted any additional public access.

Monitoring human use and related conflicts is part of ongoing management by the Wayne County Parks Department. The perimeter trail is used for equestrians and for security patrol. In other areas, horse use is monitored, and some conflicts exist between horse riders and bicycle riders who invent trails. Other, unexpected conflicts have emerged. For example, skunks (*Mephitis mephitis*), raccoons (*Procyon lotor*), minks (*Mustela vison*), and opossums (*Didelphis virginiana*) have learned to use the project's boardwalks to eat duck and bird eggs. No solution to this problem has been developed to date.

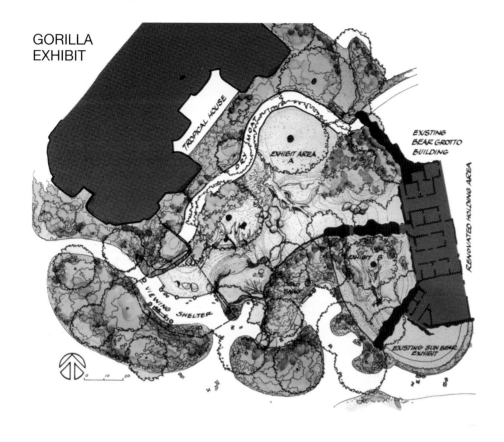

GORILLA EXHIBIT

TROPICAL HOUSE

DRY MOAT

EXHIBIT AREA A

EXISTING BEAR GROTTO BUILDING

RENOVATED HOLDING AREA

VIEWING SHELTER

EXHIBIT

EXISTING SUN BEAR EXHIBIT

0 10 20

Figure 2.2. The redesign of the lowland gorilla exhibit at Woodland Park Zoo was a seminal example of biocentric zoo design.

Source: Jones & Jones, Architects and Landscape Architects, Ltd.

Figure 2.6. Social group of lowland gorillas in the Woodland Park Zoo exhibit.

Figure 2.7. Lowland gorilla at Woodland Park Zoo.

Source for both: Jones & Jones Architects and Landscape Architects, Ltd.

Figure 2.8. Plan of the Pardisan Zoo in Tehran, Iran.

Source: Mandala Collaborative/ Wallace McHarg Roberts and Todd 1975.

Figure 2.11. Gorilla in the former primate house at Woodland Park Zoo. This inhumane and outdated exhibit concept was replaced with that of landscape immersion, in which animals are presented in social groups in a semblance of their native habitat.

Source: Jones & Jones, Architects and Landscape Architects, Ltd.

Figure 3.1. The pond system designed by CRJA (on the left) handles stormwater runoff from the federal prison complex and associated parking on the right.

Source: A Jerry Howard Photo, courtesy of Carol R. Johnson Associates, Inc. 2002.

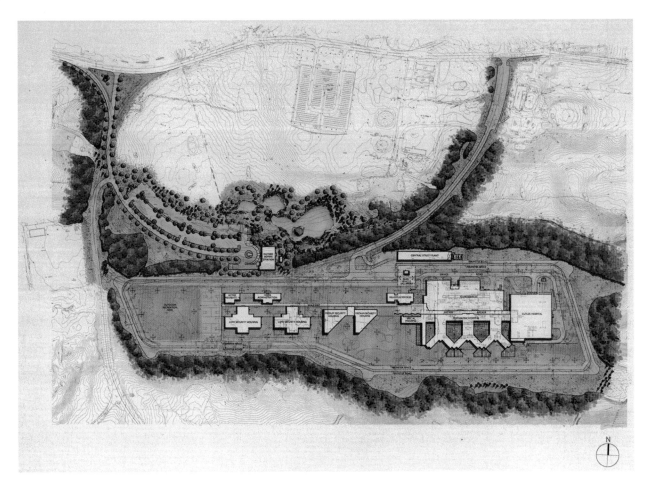

Figure 3.2. The plan of
the Devens Federal
Medical Center Complex.

*Source: Carol R. Johnson
Associates Inc. 2002.*

Figure 3.3. The deepwater pond provides wildlife habitat.

Source: A Jerry Howard photo, courtesy of Carol R. Johnson Associates, Inc. 2002.

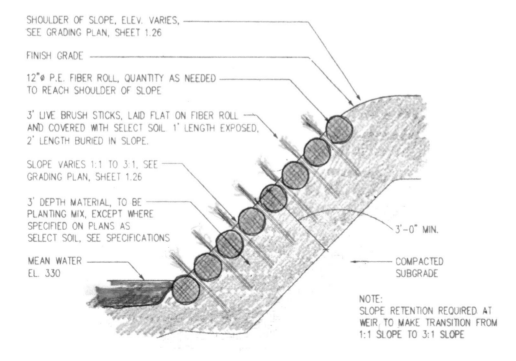

SHOULDER OF SLOPE, ELEV. VARIES,
SEE GRADING PLAN, SHEET 1.26

FINISH GRADE

12"ø P.E. FIBER ROLL, QUANTITY AS NEEDED
TO REACH SHOULDER OF SLOPE

3' LIVE BRUSH STICKS, LAID FLAT ON FIBER ROLL
AND COVERED WITH SELECT SOIL. 1' LENGTH EXPOSED,
2' LENGTH BURIED IN SLOPE.

SLOPE VARIES 1:1 TO 3:1, SEE
GRADING PLAN, SHEET 1.26

3' DEPTH MATERIAL, TO BE
PLANTING MIX, EXCEPT WHERE
SPECIFIED ON PLANS AS
SELECT SOIL, SEE SPECIFICATIONS

MEAN WATER
EL. 330

3'-0" MIN.

COMPACTED
SUBGRADE

NOTE:
SLOPE RETENTION REQUIRED AT
WEIR, TO MAKE TRANSITION FROM
1:1 SLOPE TO 3:1 SLOPE

Figure 3.4. Coir fiber logs were used to stabilize the banks of the pond system and to help establish native species.

Source: Carol R. Johnson Associates, Inc. 2002.

Figure 3.5. Coir logs were planted with native species along the banks. The weir controls the level of water in the deep pond and helps to control flooding during a one-hundred-year storm.

Source: Jack Ahern.

Figure 3.6. Large trees were preserved on the site.

Source: Jack Ahern.

Figure 4.1. The project team and client representatives at the Crosswinds Marsh Restoration Site in Wayne County, Michigan (pre-construction).

Source: Johnson Johnson & Roy/Inc.

Figure 4.2. The Crosswinds Marsh as built.

Source: Johnson Johnson & Roy/Inc.

Figure 4.3. Crosswinds
Marsh Master Plan.

*Source: Johnson Johnson &
Roy/Inc.*

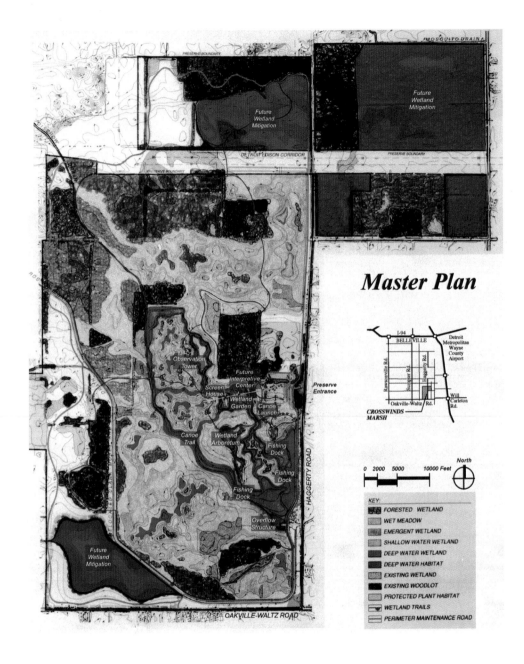

Figure 4.4. Public access and use at Crosswinds Marsh has been key to its success.

Source: Johnson Johnson & Roy/Inc.

Figure 4.5. The Crosswinds Marsh visitor and environmental education center.

Source: Johnson Johnson & Roy/Inc.

Figure 4.6. Equestrian use at Crosswinds Marsh.

Source: Johnson Johnson & Roy/Inc..

Figure 4.7. Bald eagle nesting at Crosswinds Marsh.

Source: Johnson Johnson & Roy/Inc.

Figure 4.8. ADA-accessible trails and boardwalks were provided throughout the Crosswinds marsh site as part of the public use component of the restoration plan.

Source: Johnson Johnson & Roy/Inc.

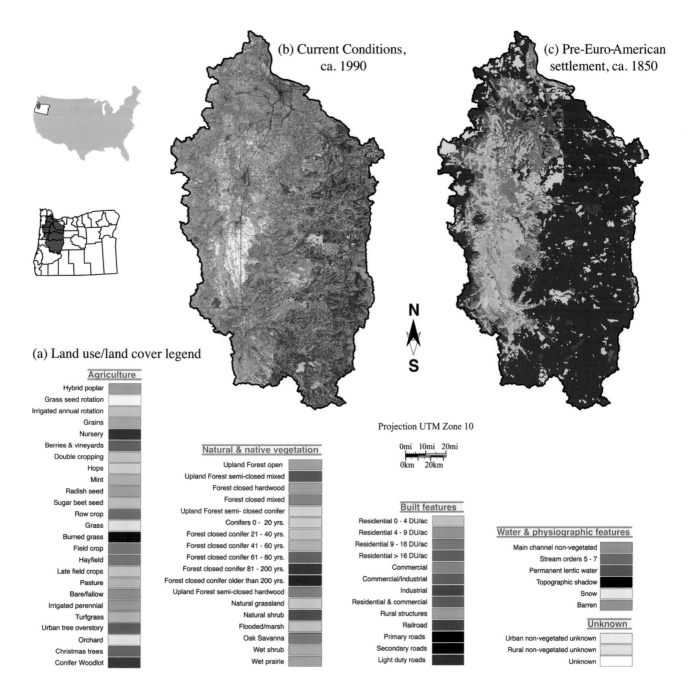

(b) Current Conditions, ca. 1990

(c) Pre-Euro-American settlement, ca. 1850

Projection UTM Zone 10

0mi 10mi 20mi

0km 20km

(a) Land use/land cover legend

Agriculture

Hybrid poplar
Grass seed rotation
Irrigated annual rotation
Grains
Nursery
Berries & vineyards
Double cropping
Hops
Mint
Radish seed
Sugar beet seed
Row crop
Grass
Burned grass
Field crop
Hayfield
Late field crops
Pasture
Bare/fallow
Irrigated perennial
Turfgrass
Urban tree overstory
Orchard
Christmas trees
Conifer Woodlot

Natural & native vegetation

Upland Forest open
Upland Forest semi-closed mixed
Forest closed hardwood
Forest closed mixed
Upland Forest semi- closed conifer
Conifers 0 - 20 yrs.
Forest closed conifer 21 - 40 yrs.
Forest closed conifer 41 - 60 yrs.
Forest closed conifer 61 - 80 yrs.
Forest closed conifer 81 - 200 yrs.
Forest closed conifer older than 200 yrs.
Upland Forest semi-closed hardwood
Natural grassland
Natural shrub
Flooded/marsh
Oak Savanna
Wet shrub
Wet prairie

Built features

Residential 0 - 4 DU/ac
Residential 4 - 9 DU/ac
Residential 9 - 16 DU/ac
Residential > 16 DU/ac
Commercial
Commercial/Industrial
Industrial
Residential & commercial
Rural structures
Railroad
Primary roads
Secondary roads
Light duty roads

Water & physiographic features

Main channel non-vegetated
Stream orders 5 - 7
Permanent lentic water
Topographic shadow
Snow
Barren

Unknown

Urban non-vegetated unknown
Rural non-vegetated unknown
Unknown

Figure 5.1. Maps comparing the land use and land cover of the pre-Euro-American settlement scenario (about 1850) (left) and that of 1990 (right). Note the dramatic reduction in old-growth forest cover (shown in dark green on the 1850 map).

Source: Hulse et al. 2004. Copyright 2004 by the Ecological Society of America.

Figure 5.3. Maps comparing the three alternative futures developed: Plan Trend 2050, Development 2050, and Conservation 2050.

Source: Hulse et al. 2004, courtesy of the Ecological Society of America.

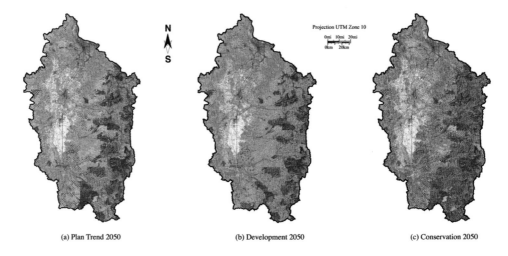

(a) Plan Trend 2050

(b) Development 2050

(c) Conservation 2050

Figure 5.5. The PATCH model overlays species habitat needs with their life-history data to determine source and sink areas for particular species. In this case, map C indicates source (red) and sink (green) areas for Cooper's hawk (*Accipiter cooperii*). White areas cannot support breeding populations.

Source: Reproduced with permission from The Williamette River Basin Atlas *published by Oregon State University Press, copyright 2002.*

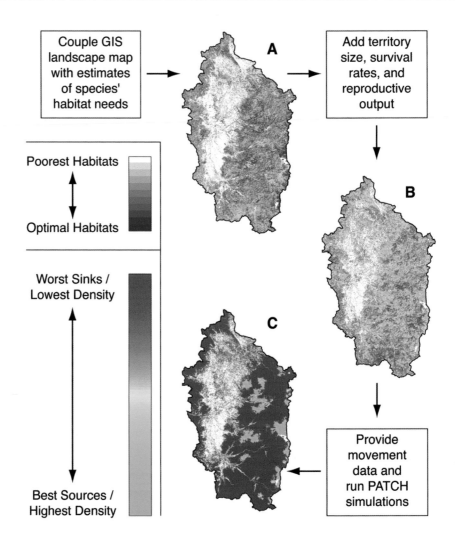

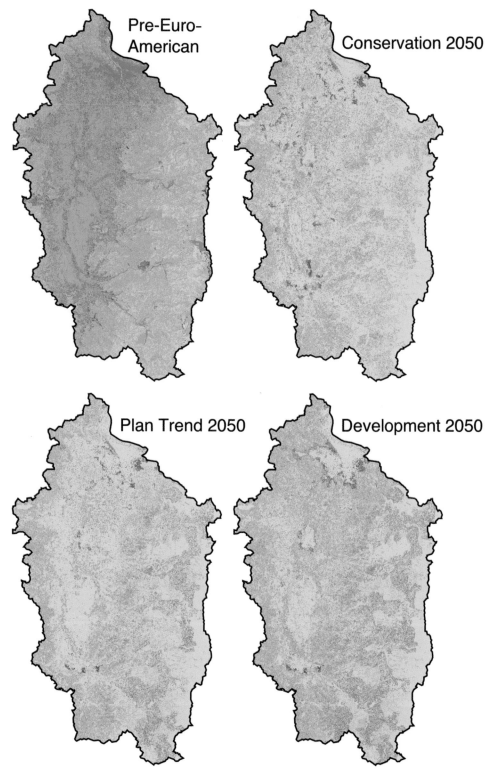

Figure 5.7. Data about changes in biodiversity are translated into maps depicting the spatial patterns of the number of species gained or lost for each scenario. Orange indicates loss of species diversity. The Development 2050 scenario depicts far greater species loss than either Plan Trend 2050 or Conservation 2050 as compared to pre-Euro-American settlement times.

Source: Reproduced with permission from The Willamette River Basin Planning Atlas, published by Oregon State University Press, copyright 2002.

Figure 5.9. Areas of influence considered in evaluating the effects of land use and land cover on stream condition: watershed (red), 393-foot (120 meter) stream buffer (also known as the riparian network).

Source: Reproduced with permission from The Willamette River Basin Planning Atlas, *published by Oregon State University Press, copyright 2002.*

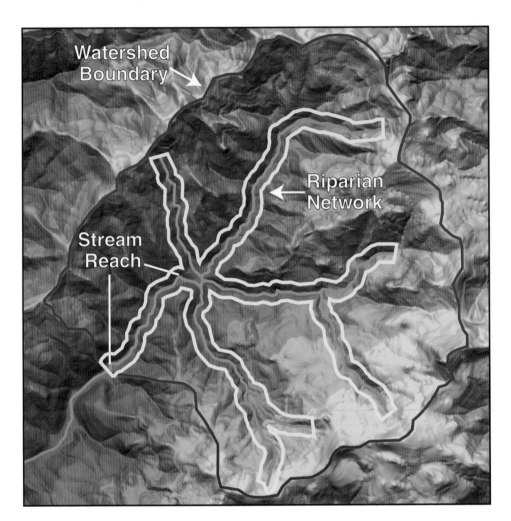

Design Concept

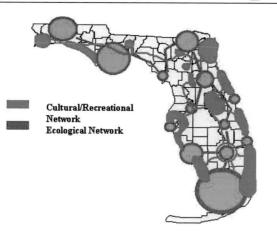

Cultural/Recreational
Network
Ecological Network

Figure 6.1. A concept for Florida's Statewide Greenways System.

Source: University of Florida, Dept. of Landscape Architecture, 1999. Executive Summary–the Florida Statewide Greenways Planning Project.

Figure 6.2. The Florida Ecological Network 2004.

Source: T. Hoctor et al. 2004.

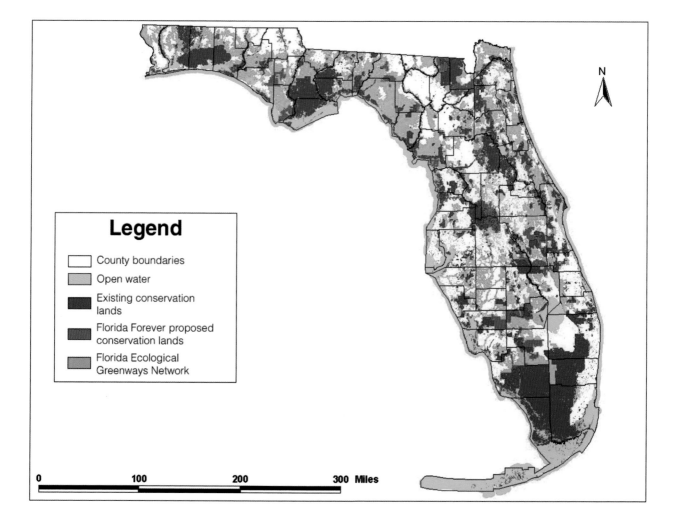

Legend

- County boundaries
- Open water
- Existing conservation lands
- Florida Forever proposed conservation lands
- Florida Ecological Greenways Network

0   100   200   300 Miles

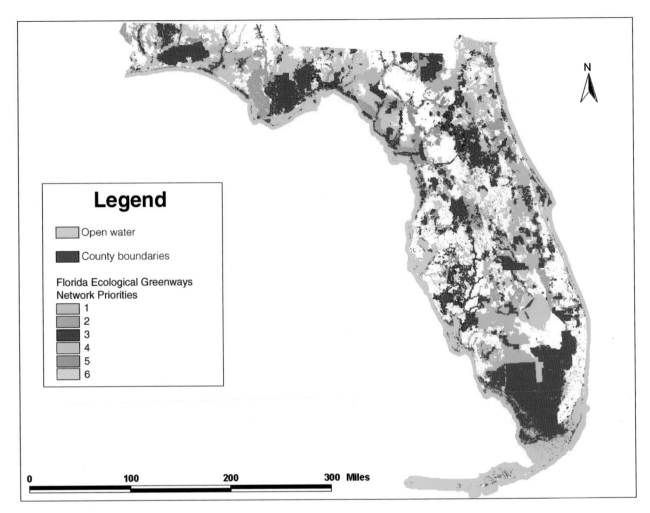

Figure 6.3. The Florida
Ecological Network
Priorities.

*Source: T. Hoctor, M. Carr, and J.
Teisinger, 2005.*

CHAPTER 5

WILLAMETTE VALLEY ALTERNATIVE FUTURES PROJECT

The Willamette River Basin is located in western Oregon between the Coast Range and the Cascade Range. The basin faces the formidable challenge of finding a way to accommodate population growth while preserving and improving valued ecological and environmental resources. The basin is a hotbed for biodiversity issues; the watershed is home to a diverse array of plant and animal species, seventeen of which are listed under the Endangered Species Act, including the northern spotted owl (*Strix occidentalis caurina*), spring Chinook salmon (*Oncorhynchus tshawytscha*), and upper Willamette River steelhead *Oncorhynchus mykiss*. However, population growth in the Willamette River Basin exceeds national rates, and the region is expected to double its current population by 2050 (Hulse 2002).

The *Oregonian* ran several articles in 2001 sponsored by the Williamette Livability Forum documenting how the economic base of the region is changing from agriculture toward technology and the service sector, resulting in many rural areas losing population while suburban and urban centers are bursting at the seams with new residents. At the same time, the region has a history of making pro-environment choices. Oregon was the first state in the nation to pass statewide land use planning and growth management legislation. This legislation grew in part from the work of landscape architect Lawrence Halprin, specifically in the book *The Willamette Valley: Choices for the Future* (Lawrence Halprin and Associates 1972). Other examples of Oregon's commitment to preserving the environment include the Oregon Forest Practices Act, passed in 1971, and the Northwest Forest Plan.

However, preserving biodiversity is but one goal that must be balanced with other pressing issues, such as water availability and land use conflicts. Fortunately, former Oregon governor (Governor 1995–2003) John Kitzhaber understood that the environment and biodiversity are integral parts of the entire system. As Kitzhaber said in a 2001 address to the Willamette Valley Livability Forum (WVLF): "The future is not a matter of chance, it is a matter of choice. It is not a thing to be waited for, it is a thing to be achieved" (Baker and Landers 2004, 311).

The Willamette Alternative Futures Project (WAFP) takes a basinwide approach to creating future scenarios that illustrate how different planning and policy decisions might affect biodiversity, water quality resources, and population over the next fifty years. Paul Risser, president of Oregon State University, thinks alternative future scenarios are "the most compelling tools to show possibilities for decision making" (Risser 2002).

PROJECT DATA

The Willamette River Basin encompasses nearly 7.4 million acres (30,000 square kilometers) of land, ranging from the steeply ridged, conifer-covered slopes of the Cascade Range to the lush, intensely forested slopes of the Coast Ranges in western Oregon and including the highly productive agricultural land of the Willamette Valley in between. The watershed varies in elevation from 1 to 10,500 feet (1 to 3,200 meters) above sea level and touches thirteen of the thirty-six counties in Oregon (Hulse 2002). The urban centers of Portland, Salem, Eugene/Springfield, and Corvallis are all within the Willamette River Basin, and demographic data indicate that all of these urban areas are suffering growing pains as they swell within their carefully delineated urban growth boundaries (Weitz and Moore 1998). Residents who consider the quality of the environment and the extensive wildland as key factors in making the valley a special place to live are concerned that growth will soon destroy what they love about the basin.

The region's land cover has undergone significant change since presettlement times. Historically, up to 75 percent of the upland forest in the basin was composed of old-growth conifers, while the lowlands were covered with Oregon white oak savannah (*Querous garryana*) or black cottonwood (*Populus balsamifera*), Oregon ash (*Fraxiaus latifolia*), and other riparian species along the Willamette River (Figure 5.1 in color insert). Development has precipitated dramatic declines of old-growth forest and Oregon white oak savannah. Through losses to urbanization and farmland, only 20 percent of the original riparian land remains forested today, and a mere 3 percent of wet and dry prairie and 5 percent of presettlement wetlands remain. In addition, modifications to and demands on the Willamette River and its tributaries have shortened the total river length by 25 percent, causing considerable habitat loss and drawdown problems (Hulse, Gregory, and Baker 2002). Significant wildlife habitat has been lost within the river and its associated streams as dams, pollution, loss of channel diversity, and sedimentation have taken their toll. The river is currently on the Clean Water Act 303(d) list for water quality violations; particular reaches have been found to contain high levels of PCPs and dioxin, and the polluted section of the river that runs through Portland is listed as a Superfund site (Willamette Riverkeeper 2002).

The WAFP included three phases. The first was to assemble and analyze current (circa 1990) and historical (circa 1850) data on the landform, water resources, biotic systems, human population, land use, and land cover aspects of the basin (Baker et al. 2004). The second phase involved diagramming three alternative future scenarios for the region that were grounded in these data, each of which worked under different land-development assumptions (Figure 5.2 and Table 5.1). The three scenarios were constrained to the same projected population increase of 3.9 million people by 2050, but one projected growth according to current trends (Plan Trend 2050), one (Conservation 2050) assumed that conservation measures in the valley would be increased, and one (Development 2050) modeled what would occur if the region relaxed its conservation restrictions in favor of development (Figure 5.3 in color insert; see also Figure 5.4) (Hulse 2002). During the third phase, investigators modeled the effects of these alternate futures on four core areas of concern: (1) the ecological condition of the Willamette River, (2) water availability, (3) the ecological condition of streams associated with the river, and (4) terrestrial wildlife (Hulse 2002; Baker et al. 2004; Schumaker et al. 2004; Van Sickle et al. 2004).

PROJECT PARTICIPANTS

The WAFP is a regional venture that began in 1995. The project was triggered by then-U.S. president Bill Clinton's Northwest Forest Plan (Willamette Valley Livability Forum 2001). In response to the plan, the U.S. Environmental Protection Agency (EPA) initiated a research plan headed by Joan Baker, an EPA ecologist, calling for the creation of the Pacific Northwest Ecosystem Research Consortium, an assemblage of thirty-four scientists from ten institutions, including the EPA, Oregon State University, University

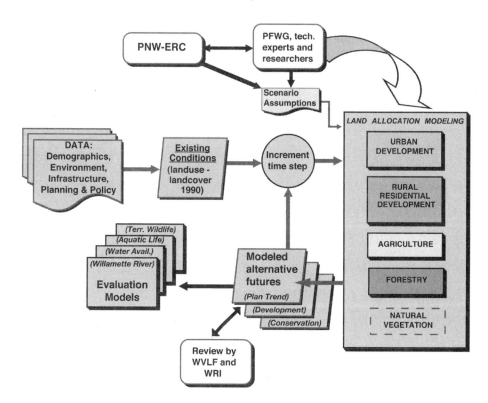

Scenario Development Process

Figure 5.2. The scenario development model of the Willamette Alternative Futures Project (WAFP) illustrates how data were incorporated into models and at what point project participants' decisions were used to formulate alternative future development. Land allocation modeling derived from Pacific Northwest Ecosystem Resource Consortium (PNW-ERC) scenario assumptions was combined with existing data to build the three alternative scenarios.

Source: Reproduced with permission from The Willamette River Basin Planning Atlas published by Oregon State University Press, copyright 2002.

Scenario	Strategy	Effect on Farmland or Forestry	Effect on Terrestrial and Aquatic Wildlife Species	Effect on Urban Areas	Effect on Water Resources
Conservation 2050	Ecosystem protection and restoration prioritized within plausible limits	15 percent of prime farmland lost to natural vegetation; 17 percent increase in older conifer forest	31 percent more terrestrial wildlife species gain habitat than lose habitat	New development only in UGB* with emphasis on high density; amount of urbanized land increases by 18 percent	Surface water consumption up 43 percent; 70 percent increase in stream length that runs dry during summer
Plan Trend 2050	Current policies and trends continue	Less than 2 percent total land area lost, but 19 percent decline in older conifer forest	Small basin-wide effects (10 percent change from 1990) but some significant specific declines	New development only in UGB; population density doubles to 18 residents/hectare. amount of urbanized land increases by 25 percent. 8.3 percent land area covered by urban, suburban, and rural development, (23.9 percent increase over 1990 levels)	Surface water consumption up 57 percent; significant effects on stream flow for second to fourth order streams: doubling stream length that runs dry during summer
Development 2050	Loosening of current policies to reflect more market-oriented approach	24 percent loss of prime land; 22 percent decline in older conifer forest	Large basin-wide effects (39 percent more species lose habitant than gain over 1990 levels) no significant effects for aquatic life	Significant population growth in UGBs up to 14.6 residents/hectare; amount of urbanized land increases by 50 percent; 10.4 percent land area covered by urban, suburban. and rural development. A 55.2 percent increase over 1990 levels	Surface water consumption up 58 percent; significant effects on stream flow for second to fourth order streams: 75 percent increase in stream length that runs dry during moderate summer

* Urban Growth Boundary (UGB)

Table 5.1. The three alternative futures make varying land use assumptions and have different implications for forestry, farmland, aquatic and terrestrial life, urban areas, and water resources. The Conservation 2050 plan assumes stricter environmental controls and the prioritizing of habitat preservation. The Plan Trend 2050 scenario works within current trends, while the Development 2050 scenario assumes a more market-based, prodevelopment climate. The scenarios were intended to inform affected citizens and decision makers of the likely effects of alternative planning policies.

Source: adapted from Hulse, Gregory, and Baker 2002.

of Oregon, University of Washington, and U.S. Forest Service. The consortium included experts from a diverse array of disciplines, including terrestrial and aquatic ecology, hydrology, landscape architecture, limnology, geography, forestry, remote sensing, ecological statistics, agronomy, and computer modeling (Hulse 2002).

The consortium provided scientific data from a variety of fields to support community-based environmental planning through the WVLF and the Willamette

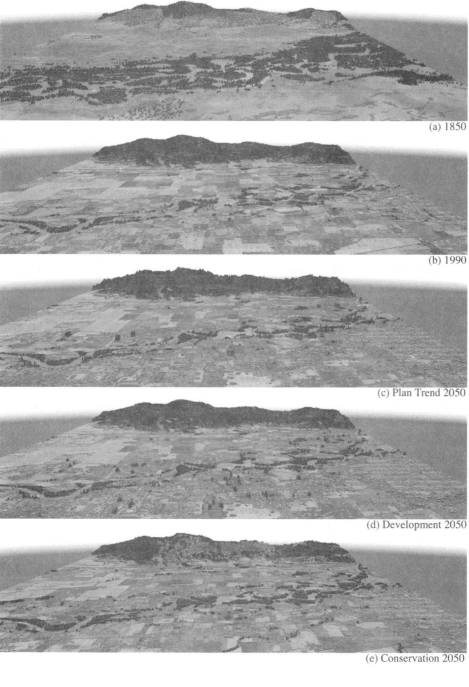

(a) 1850

(b) 1990

(c) Plan Trend 2050

(d) Development 2050

(e) Conservation 2050

Figure 5.4. Visualizations of the past, present, and three alternative futures for a portion of the southern Willamette Basin north of Eugene. Note the reduction in channel complexity and floodplain forest compared with the 1850 map as well as the differential spread of urbanization under the three future scenarios.

Source: Reproduced with permission from The Williamette River Basin Planning Atlas, *published by Oregon State University Press, copyright 2002.*

Restoration Initiative (WRI) now called the Willamette Partnership (Hulse 2002). The WVLF formed in 1996 with the goal of creating planning strategies based on development, conservation, and restoration concerns. Two years later, in 1998, the WRI was established with the task of outlining strategies to conserve and restore wildlife habitat, protect endangered species, address water quality issues, and manage floodplains while also considering human population projections. The two groups were carefully selected to represent the diverse interests in the river basin, including tribal leaders, private citizens, industry and business spokespersons, members of nongovernmental organizations, and representatives from local, state, and federal governments (Hulse 2002). The project is funded by the EPA through a cooperative agreement with Oregon State University and the Pacific Northwest Ecosystem Research Consortium.

Landscape architects have participated in Oregon's regional planning efforts for many years. The WAFP is rooted in an early publication by Lawrence Halprin (1972) that was deemed "The Coloring Book" because it empowered groups to create their own development scenarios by completing a matrix of cross influences of land use and other uses. The book helped change land use policy and planning in Oregon in the 1970s as it fueled adoption of the statewide planning act, Senate Bill 100, in 1973, which established statewide planning and mandatory municipal plans (Lawrence Halprin and Associates 1972).

Landscape architects and planners played a central coordinating role in the WAFP. David Hulse and his colleagues at the University of Oregon were the lead landscape architects on this project. According to ecologist Joan Baker, Hulse was a crucial leader in the venture, providing a broad-scale perspective while the group was designing for the future. Hulse acted as the integrator for the multidisciplinary team and also conveyed project ideas and objectives to communities (Baker 2002). According to Sara Vickerman, a consortium member from Defenders of Wildlife, Hulse's experience with a breadth of disciplines helped him bridge the gap between scientific information and application (Bastach, Gregory, and Vickerman 2002).

To succeed, projects like the WAFP must find ways to convey data and issues to a local audience. In the WAFP, as in similar projects, producing quality data was not enough to effect change; the data needed to be packaged in a powerful, user-friendly, visual medium in order to influence the public (Bastach, Gregory, and Vickerman 2002; Hulse, Branscomb, and Payne 2004). Biologist Paul Risser believes that the key contribution of landscape architects and planners to biodiversity planning is their practical ability to bring human and social views into the discussion while simultaneously working with sophisticated data analysis tools (Risser 2002). Rick Bastach, of the Willamette Restoration Initiative, describes the landscape architects of the WAFP as the "managers" of the public participation process, while Stan Gregory, consortium ecologist from Oregon State University and the Department of Fisheries and Wildlife, credits them for their willingness to dig into the science and for allowing affected citizens to set the assumptions. According to Gregory, the landscape architects applied their understanding of the target audience to devising graphics that placed understandable information in front of the public (Bastach, Gregory, and Vickerman 2002).

Hulse made the pivotal decision of how best to represent the alternative futures in ways that the public would understand. Understanding that the public responds well to animated visualizations, his team used graphic techniques to distill the data so members of the public could easily review the scenarios (Hulse, Branscomb, and Payne 2004). In Hulse's opinion, the project is more likely to succeed because it is both scientifically defensible and conceptually accessible to the public (Hulse 2002).

PROJECT GOALS AND OBJECTIVES

The three-part entity composed of the WVLF, the WRI (now the Williamette Partnership), and the Pacific Northwest Ecosystem Research Consortium (the Consortium) worked together to fulfill its goal of developing integrated strategies for development and conservation within the Willamette Valley in the face of projected rapid population growth. The Consortium's specific goal was to provide scientific information to help policy makers and citizens make better choices concerning local and regional land and water use. They wanted to help shape the WVLF's image of the basin's future, aid in the WRI's basinwide restoration strategy, and help local citizens and governments make more informed decisions.

The Consortium's research centered on these four objectives:

1. Discovering how humans had altered the natural resources of the basin in the last 150 years.
2. Projecting how humans might change the landscape in the future given a range of possibilities.
3. Determining expected environmental effects from these changes.
4. Revealing which actions in which specific locations within the basin would have the greatest effects on natural resources (Hulse 2002; Schumaker et al. 2004; Van Sickle et al. 2004).

The scientists in the Consortium also tailored their models to achieving the biodiversity goals of preserving and restoring functioning ecosystems rather than simply focusing on species. The goal of the landscape architects working within the Consortium was to present the complex data regarding patterns and trends in the basin to the public in a clear, easily understood manner. The WVLF and the WRI worked to achieve their objective of including as much community participation in the process as possible. All of these objectives combined to help move the project toward its overall goals.

PUBLIC/PRIVATE PARTNERSHIP AND COLLABORATION

Politicians require a certain level of assurance that their constituents are invested in the process of change before they will support controversial measures, such as investing in land acquisition for restoration or conservation. The members of the Consortium, the

WVLF, and the WRI knew that involving community representatives early in the process would help ensure that the project results would be credible to politicians (Bastach, Gregory, and Vickerman 2002). Community participation was an integral part of the process throughout the Willamette Alternative Futures Project. After the Consortium determined the project goals, they organized a "Possible Futures Working Group," consisting of twenty citizens from diverse backgrounds representing real estate, farming, planning, transportation, metropolitan, industry, and environmental interests. This group had the task of testing assumptions and formulating three realistic future development paths for the basin (Willamette Valley Livability Forum 2001). The group's objective was to plan for multiple uses in the spirit of Oregon's statewide planning initiative. Thus, they considered a full suite of land uses and actions and explicitly addressed which types of land uses would be prioritized for different locations. They met with the Consortium monthly for two years, and then the Consortium reviewed the details with the WVLF and the WRI before creating models to both generate and evaluate the scenarios (Hulse 2002).

Investigators in the WAFP champion a philosophy of public involvement in the biodiversity planning process. They understand that the United States' population increase and the resultant intensifying and spread of land use pose the greatest threats to ecosystem sustainability and biodiversity. They believe that mitigating these effects requires changing the behavior of large numbers of people, and they contend that top-down governmental regulation approaches are ineffective because of deeply held values regarding individual rights to property and wealth (Hulse 2000). Instead, the investigators advocate for design solutions derived from a partnership between government agencies and community residents—a process that produces greater understanding among the participants and a higher probability that the Futures Project's results will be used (Baker 2002).

The process of involving a public–private collaboration in the WAFP enabled the public to share in a vision for shaping the future that is not an all-or-nothing scenario. For example, as noted by Sara Vickerman, community members were amazed to realize that wildlife prospects can improve despite human population growth (Bastach, Gregory, and Vickerman 2002).

BIODIVERSITY DATA ISSUES

The WAFP takes a multispecies, landscape-level approach to biodiversity. The project is unique in that it examines both terrestrial and aquatic biodiversity under the umbrella of one large study and it develops predictive models to simulate how the three scenarios would likely affect biodiversity in the region. In developing the models, investigators searched for a middle ground between pragmatism and biological realism while coping with incomplete wildlife life-history data.

The project used GIS maps of pre-Euro-American settlement and 1990 conditions to catalog habitat. The scientists also used data from the Nature Conservancy, the Oregon Natural Heritage Program, and GAP analysis (Hulse 2002). The project approaches biodiversity by weighing the importance of all species equally. Endangered species were selected not for their endangered status but rather because significant life-history data were available for these species (Schumaker et al. 2004). The project took both a reactive and a proactive approach to biodiversity. Project biologists analyzed species richness throughout the basin and modeled how different species respond to landscape change (Hulse, Gregory, and Baker 2002). While developing scenarios, they tried to avoid creating designs that placed development in the major source areas for particular species, but they also identified high-priority areas to restore. Also, while generating models, they focused more on habitats, on the variety of life and its process-es, as opposed to individual species occurrences.

The project assessed terrestrial wildlife with both a simple method and a more complex approach. For the simple method, the biologists identified and examined thirty-four habitat types for each of 279 amphibian, reptile, bird, and mammal species occurring now and historically in the Willamette River Basin. They permitted viable habitat to represent species viability and ranked species for each habitat type (Schumaker et al. 2004). This approach is limited, as habitat does not always correlate exactly with true population levels. Consequently, the researchers extended the analysis for a subset of 17 species for which they had adequate data by developing the PATCH model (Program to Assist in Tracking Critical Habitat), which incorporated the effects of habitat quality, quantity, and pattern on species life history parameters, such as survival rates, fecundi-ty, and migration. (See Table 5.2 for a list of species used in PATCH analysis.) The PATCH model diagrams where wildlife species should occur and at what densities they can be expected to viably exist (Figure 5.5 in color insert). When coupled with the simple approach, PATCH highlights landscape connectivity implications for wildlife (Hulse, Gregory, and Baker 2002).

The study results demonstrated some counterintuitive findings, such as when a large population increase resulted from a small gain in habitat quality, as with the western meadowlark (*Sturnella neglecta*) under the Conservation 2050 scenario. This is clear evidence of landscape fragmentation's effect on biodiversity. Overall, the PATCH data indicated that populations for the seventeen species declined under both the Plan Trend and the Development scenarios, with species suffering 10 percent and 39 percent loss-es, respectively (Figure 5.6 and Figure 5.7 in color insert). In contrast, the Conservation scenario demonstrated a 31 percent increase in the number of species gaining habitat (Hulse 2002). Hulse writes: "For wildlife species already stressed by habitat loss and fragmentation, this

Table 5.2. List of Species Used in PATCH Analysis for Wildlife in the Willamette Alternative Futures Project.

Source: Hulse, Gregory, and Baker 2002, 127.

Common Name	Scientific Name
blue grouse	*Dendragapus obscurus*
bobcat	*Lynx rufus*
cooper's hawk	*Accipiter cooperii*
coyote	*Canis latrans*
black-capped chickadee	*Parus atricapillus*
douglas squirrel	*Tamiasciurus douglasii mollipilosus*
gray jay	*Perisoreus Canadensis*
great horned owl	*Bubo virginianus*
marsh wren	*Cistothorus palustris*
mourning dove	*Zenaida macoura*
northern goshawk	*Accipiter gentiles*
northern spotted owl	*Strix occidentalis caurina*
pileated woodpecker	*Dryocopus pileatus*
raccoon	*Procyon lotor*
red fox	*Vulpes vulpes*
red-tailed hawk	*Buteo jamaicensis*
western meadowlark	*Sturnella neglecta*

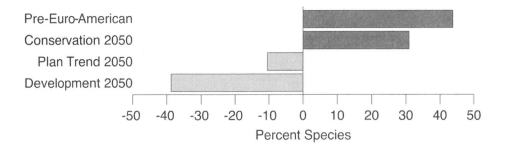

Figure 5.6. The models show the percentages of the total species studied that lost (light gray) or gained (dark gray) habitat under the three scenarios and for pre-Euro-American settlement levels, using current habitat levels as a reference point. The net 40 percent difference between the Conservation 2050 scenario and the Plan Trend 2050 scenario highlights the potential effectiveness of biodiversity planning. According to the models, if current planning and land use trends continue, 10 percent of species in the basin will lose habitat by 2050.

Source: Reproduced with permission from The Willamette River Basin Planning Atlas, *published by Oregon State University Press, copyright 2002.*

work suggests the choice between alternative futures may be critical to their long-term likelihood of persistence" (Hulse, Gregory, and Baker 2002, 127).

The WAFP not only examined effects on terrestrial species but predicted how land use decisions affect aquatic systems. The study used several tools to measure the aquatic conditions in 130 stream reaches associated with the river. They first examined native fish richness (the number of native species) and developed a fish Index of Biotic Integrity to compare the overall integrity of fish in the basin with historic reference levels (Figure 5.8). They also examined the richness and referenced condition of invertebrate populations in the river using EPT—Ephemeroptera (mayfly), Plecoptera (stonefly), Trichoptera (caddisfly)—monitoring and the Willamette Invertebrate Observed/Expected Index. Finally, they mapped land use and land cover data for four different "zones of influence" for each stream reach, ranging from the large scale (the watershed) to the local scale (the 393-foot [120 meter] riparian zone immediately bordering a reach) (Figure 5.9 in color insert; Hulse 2002; Van Sickle et al. 2004).

All of these data were compiled into models that statistically determined relationships between stream indicators and land uses. The models were then combined with stream flow data generated by models that took agricultural, reservoir, and other watershed effects into account. The resultant models predicted the effects of land use and land cover changes on stream habitat quality and demonstrated that major impacts occur when riparian vegetation is changed to agriculture or urban/residential development (Figure 5.9 in color insert) (Hulse 2002).

POSTPROJECT EVALUATION

It is difficult to explicitly measure the effect of the Willamette Alternative Futures Project. The participants view the scenarios as guides and do not expect any one of the three scenarios to be wholly accepted as a plan for the future. Rather, they intended to focus attention on issues and to demonstrate the implications of planning decisions to help forge a consensus among stakeholders on goals, priorities, targets, and strategic approaches (Baker et al. 2004). However, they have tried to assess whether they met their goals of providing valid, usable data to the public to facilitate planning. For example, a conference sponsored by the Willamette Valley Livability Forum at Oregon State University in April 2001 to spur public interest featured the results of the study (Risser 2002).

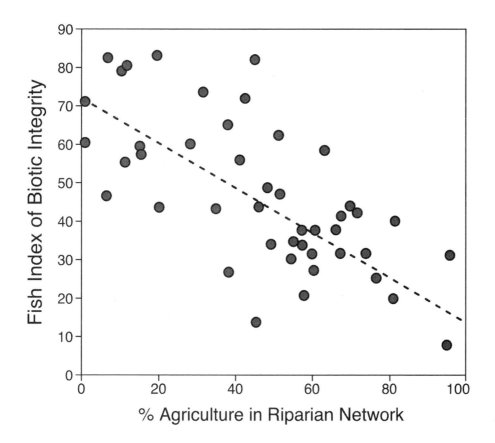

Figure 5.8. The Index of Biotic Integrity (IBI) is a measure of the influence of agriculture on stream quality. The overall health of fish populations in selected streams was compared with historic data from those same streams. Higher IBI numbers indicate streams with healthier fish populations. The graph shows that as the amount of land used for agriculture increases the health of fish populations decreases in a linear fashion. This inverse relationship provides sound evidence that intensive land use is potentially harmful to biodiversity.

Source: Reproduced with permission from The Willamette River Basin Planning Atlas, published by Oregon State University Press, copyright 2002.

The study results also reached 450,000 households in the basin through an eight-page feature titled "The Future Is in Our Hands," which ran in the *Willamette Chronicle* newspaper in 2001. This feature delivered the basic findings of the three alternative futures to a large audience and rapidly educated many people about the status of development in the valley. In the insert, Paul Risser celebrates the findings of the WAFP as he states: "With careful and deliberate efforts, we can accommodate growth while also recapturing 20–65 percent of the natural ecological function we have lost during the past 150 years of intensive use of the Willamette River Basin's natural resources." The public can also access the results of the study on the Internet and through a published atlas (Hulse, Gregory, and Baker 2002).

Clearly, the Willamette Alternative Futures Project met its goals of providing useful data to a wide audience. WAFP findings and methods have also been used in the Willamette Restoration Initiative's restoration strategy, during 1000 Friends of Oregon's process of examining future infrastructure costs for developing commercial land, and by the Alternative Transportation Futures Project, funded by the Federal Highway Administration and the Oregon Department of Transportation. The study has also catalyzed the organization of many new local watershed councils; the State now recognizes more than thirty of these councils (Hulse 2002). These data have also been successfully incorporated into the planning strategies of organizations that have the power to effect change at a landscape level, such as the Federal Highway Administration.

No biological monitoring was done to validate the visual projections of the scenarios after they were completed. Viewing such monitoring as a future step that would add credence to the work, Stan Gregory wants the Consortium to create a monitoring program. He envisions a regional environmental observation akin to a "Hubble telescope turned inward" that tracks changes in ownership and land management in the basin to see if the trajectories are realized (Bastach, Gregory, and Vickerman 2002). Also, although the scientists involved in generating data on biodiversity were focused on communities and ecosystems, they are now trying to bring a specific species-oriented approach back to the work by looking at species-specific issues, such as the current public concern over the meadowlark (*Sturnella neglecta*) (Bastach, Gregory, and Vickerman 2002).

The team tried to respond to public concerns about making scientific research more relevant to real-world applications, but project participants ran into many conflicts as they constructed their models. Under the Conservation 2050 scenario, water became a hotly debated commodity; more river water for fish meant less water for agriculture. Clashes of interest also arose over the possible location of designated restoration areas. For example, when experts selected sites to restore fire-dependent oak savannah habitat, they ran into problems locating a new highway (Baker 2002). In addition, as noted by Sara Vickerman, the lack of a basinwide political entity became a major obstacle in implementing the project findings (Bastach, Gregory, and Vickerman 2002). However, the time requirement for such a process is a common drawback of community participation. The scientists also cited the public's difficulty in brainstorming for creative options and their reluctance to consider futures with far-reaching changes from existing policies. Joan Baker sees this as limiting the spectrum of outcomes for the three scenarios, and she advocates bringing in expert-based designs early to inspire citizen's ideas about alternatives (Baker 2002).

FLORIDA STATEWIDE GREENWAYS SYSTEM PLANNING PROJECT

The state of Florida loses more than 120,000 acres (50,000 hectares) of rural land to development each year (Hoctor et al. 2004). In response to this trend in development, the Florida legislature supported a statewide greenways and trail system.

The role of greenways and trails in maintaining the integrity of natural landscapes and ecosystems has been explored by many, including Charles Flink, R. Searns, adn L. Schwartz, in *Greenways: A Guide to Planning Design and Development* (1993), and Charles Little, in *Greenways for America* (1995). Although more complex definitions exist, for the purposes of this chapter the term greenway is defined as "a corridor of protected open space that is managed for conservation and/or recreation" (Executive Summary FDEP&FGCC 1998).

The University of Florida's Departments of Landscape Architecture and Planning was integral in researching and designing the greenways plan. The project used an integrated landscape approach to "ensure that a diversity of natural and cultural resource issues were taken into consideration," incorporating such characteristics as applying at multiple scales, addressing systemwide rather than site-specific features, involving multiple stakeholders and disciplines, and considering context (University of Florida 1999). Many of these characteristics correspond closely to this case study's suggestions as to how landscape architects approach the issue of biodiversity in their work.

PROJECT DATA

The Florida Statewide Greenways System Planning Project began in 1995 as a continuation of work undertaken by the Florida Greenways Commission in 1993–94. The project was prepared at the statewide scale and broken down into two subsystems: the Ecological Network and the Recreational/Cultural Network (Figure 6.1) (University of Florida 1999). For this case study, with its emphasis on biodiversity planning, we will focus almost exclusively on the development of the Florida Ecological Network (FEN), although the two networks are not isolated systems.

The project was developed in phases from 1995 to 1998; in 1999, an action plan called *Connecting Florida's Communities with Greenways and Trails: The Five Year Implementation Plan for the Florida Greenway and Trails System* was adopted by the legislature. Implementation of the FEN has been underway ever since, including identification of priority areas to strategically focus conservation efforts. The project team at the University of Florida has been updating the FEN to reflect conservation achievements and land use changes since its inception. Despite the ongoing nature of the project, this discussion focuses on the period from 1995 to 1999, when the first statewide greenways plan was delineated.

The Florida Ecological Network was initially developed to comply with several mandates set forth by Florida statutes. Most critically, statutory language was adopted declaring the legislature's intent to establish and expand a statewide system of greenways and trails to be designated as "Florida's Greenways and Trail System." Legislatively mandated steps toward that end included (1) designating the Florida Department of Environmental Protection (FDEP) as the lead state agency, and (2) creating the Florida Greenways Coordinating Council (FGCC) to help the FDEP. Required actions included preparing a five-year plan, adopting benchmarks to measure implementation progress, and compiling management recommendations for the greenways system (for more information, see Florida Department of Environmental Protection and Florida Greenways Coordinating Council 1998).

Funding for the project—about $1.2 million from 1995 to 1999—came primarily from the Florida Department of Transportation's (FDOT's) share of U.S. federal Intermodal Surface Transportation Efficiency Act (ISTEA) funds. For the past fifty years, 4.8 miles (3 kilometers) of new highway have been built per day in Florida. Obviously, this level of construction strongly affects ecosystems and biodiversity, and the FDOT was looking for ways to minimize these impacts (Hoctor et al. 2004). The FDOT was interested in this particular project because it wanted to identify landscape resources to be avoided when building roads and to explore the possibility of using trails as an alternate mode of transportation (Carr 2002). As the lead agency, the FDEP also provided some funding.

PROJECT PARTICIPANTS

This project was a continuation of efforts begun in 1991 by the Conservation Fund and 1,000 Friends of Florida, when these groups created the Florida Greenways Project in an attempt to build a statewide constituency for greenways. They also initiated several greenways and trails prototype projects at the community and regional levels. In 1993, Governor Lawton Chiles created the Florida Greenways Commission (FGC) in response to this effort. The commission was charged with determining whether the greenways concept had a place in public policy and, if so, what principles were critical for effective implementation. In their 1994 report to the governor, the FGC affirmed a belief that greenways could enhance Florida's efforts to conserve its natural and cultural heritage as well as its commitment to outdoor recreation. The FGC provided recommendations for a greenways system to link natural areas and open space, conserve native landscapes and ecosystems, and increase recreational opportunities for citizens and visitors. In response to this report, the Florida legislature created the FGCC in 1995 to continue the work of the commission and to assist the FDEP in policy implementation. The FGCC was a twenty-six-member board composed of public and private representatives of business, conservation, landowner, recreation, and local and federal government interests as well as state agency representatives (FDEP & FGCC 1998).

In 1995, after the greenways legislation had been adopted, the University of Florida was asked to prepare a recommended design/physical plan for the greenways system. This plan was developed using a geographic information system (GIS) decision support model (DSM) to help identify high-priority conservation areas for the FEN. By overlaying multiple data layers (representing, for example, roadless areas, land use and land cover, and species habitats) to create a map of priority conservation areas, the GIS model provided a sound scientific basis on which to identify and rank ecologically sensitive areas. The project was based in the university's Department of Landscape Architecture, with strong involvement by individuals from many other university departments. The principal investigators were Margaret (Peggy) Carr (Professor, Department of Landscape Architecture), Mark Benedict (Associate Scientist, Department of Landscape Architecture), Thomas Hoctor (Doctoral Candidate, Department of Wildlife Ecology and Conservation), and Paul Zwick (Professor, Department of Urban and Regional Planning).

As the only landscape architect involved, Professor Peggy Carr describes her role as "assembling the team" and determining the decision-making process by which all work would be completed. Design principles were applied to bring the project and its participants together by integrating multiple interests. The process included establishing goals and objectives, analyzing and synthesizing the inventory, creating alternative scenarios, and measuring the project's progress toward achieving its goals and objectives. Professor Carr had a particular interest in the ethical basis for the project. She believes that human interaction should also be considered when planning a successful greenway because human well-being is dependent on healthy, functioning ecosystems. She considered the ideal approach as one that blended immediate human needs (e.g., for recreation opportunities) with long-term human dependency on healthy ecosystems. This, she asserts, is why the project required the involvement of a landscape architect—because the scientists involved were "hard core conservationists" focusing their attention on the ecological aspects of the project, and the recreationists were equally focused on immediate human uses of the greenway. Including a landscape architect in the plan's development brought these two sides together to create a greenway plan with multiple uses and functions (Carr 2002).

During the development of the DSM, a large technical advisory team was assembled to provide peer review and to test the model's assumptions. The team included representatives of natural resource agencies and nongovernmental organizations (NGOs). The first phase involved applying the model and generating maps of the FEN. The phase 1 results, titled "Decision Support Model Results," were publicly aired.

The second phase included citizens as well as representatives from local government, Florida's five water management districts, timber and farming interests, and conservation and recreation NGOs. Professor Carr was particularly involved in these meetings, acting as "translator" to relate technical information and attempting to help the public visualize the results of the greenway plan. The results of this second phase were called "Decision Support Model Results as Modified by Public Comment."

A third, and final, phase involved review by landowners, who were allowed to have their lands removed from state maps of the FEN if they chose. The results of the third phase of review were titled "Model Results as Modified by Public Comment and Private Landowner Comment." However, the phase two's results, "Decision Support Model Results as Modified by Public Comment," are a more complete representation of the FEN because they identify important ecological and recreational hubs and linkages (Carr 2002; Hoctor 2002; FDEP & FGCC 1998).

The Florida Ecological Network was originally adopted as the Florida Ecological Opportunities Network in 1999. It was updated in 2004 with the following changes: 1) inclusion of conservation acquisitions that occurred between 1999 and 2004, 2) exclusion of areas originally found to have conservation potential that were converted to urban use between 1999 and 2004, and 3) inclusion of some areas of pastureland not originally included because of a change in the criteria used for determining ecological potential (Figure 6.2).

Once the Florida Ecological Network 2004 was adopted by the state, it was evaluated and prioritized in 2005. Priority 1 lands are those found in large, intact patches contiguous to significant existing conservation lands. Priority 2 lands are the balance of those that if protected would provide continuous ecological connectivity from south Florida to the western panhandle. Priority 3 lands provide redundancy or enhancement to critical corridors. Priority 4 lands mostly enhance riverine protective zones in north Florida. Priority 5 lands are mostly altered agricultural lands that have potential to provide ecological connectivity but with less existing ecological integrity than higher priority area. Priority 6 lands are mostly existing working landscapes that augment or are redundant with other proposed connection (Figure 6.3).

PROJECT GOALS AND OBJECTIVES

The Florida Statewide Greenways System Planning Project was a broad-scale project that involved many participants and had a number of stated goals and objectives. The overall goal was to create a "green infrastructure" to "link natural areas and open spaces, conserving native landscapes and ecosystems and offering recreational opportunities across the state" (FDEP & FGCC 1998). After examining the goals described by the 1994 Report to the Governor, the university team developed additional goals to clarify which direction they would take. With this in mind, the overarching goal stated in the University's "Final Report, Phase II" is "to delineate a physical plan for a statewide greenways system, combining the results of GIS modeling and public input while following guidelines contained in the Florida Greenways Commission's December 1994 Report to the Governor."

The specific goals and objectives guiding the development of the Florida Ecological Network were to use a regional landscape approach to design an ecologically functioning statewide greenways system that

- conserves critical elements of Florida's native ecosystems and landscapes,
- restores and maintains connectivity among native ecological systems and processes,
- facilitates the ability of these ecosystems and landscapes to function as dynamic systems, and
- maintains the evolutionary potential of these ecosystems to adapt to future environmental changes (University of Florida 1999).

Thomas Hoctor simplified the goal of the FEN to the following: "to determine how everything fits together, thereby selecting viable areas to conserve biodiversity" (Hoctor 2002). This is a coarse filter approach that aims to protect entire ecosystems rather than focusing on individual species. In this way, both common and threatened species are protected along with their habitats. Implementing the project would maintain connectivity across the state and would conserve flora and fauna integral to Florida's natural ecosystems. This is especially important given the rapid rate of urbanization in Florida and the large number of federally listed endangered and threatened species, for which Florida ranks third in the United States.

The continued existence of some of Florida's more fragile ecosystems and species depends on a lack of disturbance. Thus, human use of these areas needs to be carefully planned and managed. Figure 6.2 shows the FEN map that resulted from the planning process. As described earlier, the greenway system needed to achieve dual purposes of conserving native landscapes and ecosystems and providing recreational opportunities for both citizens and visitors. Professor Carr describes the ecological network as a foundation on which the other parts of the system can be supported, including linear recreation and cultural heritage. It was necessary to first determine what areas should be preserved with no significant human use, and then which areas could be designated for appropriate human recreational use (Carr 2002). By following this process, particularly sensitive areas with high-priority status in terms of biodiversity could be identified and "set aside" as necessary, and other areas could be successfully used for both habitat and ecosystem protection and human recreation.

PUBLIC/PRIVATE PARTNERSHIP AND COLLABORATION

The Florida Statewide Greenways System Planning Project was a collaborative effort on many levels. The overall project was a partnership between the Department of Environmental Protection, the Florida Greenways Coordinating Council (which itself consisted of members from several different public and private sectors), the University of Florida, the Florida Department of Transportation, and many others. Public agencies, citizens, and public landowners all had a hand in developing the project's vision and, later, its recommendations.

The general public and private landowners were most directly involved in more than twenty working group sessions that followed the development of the DSM, when they thoroughly reviewed the model's "products" (Hoctor et al. 2004). The DSM was modified very little by the general public at these meetings, although landowners were able to choose to have their lands removed from the ecological network—and some did. The design of the trails network, on the other hand, was highly influenced by the public. It seems that GIS modeling was less effective for designing a statewide trails network than an ecological network, and the personal experiences and opinions of the public provided the fine-grained detail needed to design trails (Carr 2002). The Nature Conservancy, the Trust for Public Land, and 1,000 Friends of Florida were also involved in the review process.

The issue of private property rights proved to be the largest stumbling block to the project. Attorneys for some large landholders became highly involved in the review process, preventing the mapping efforts from carrying any regulatory authority. Many individual meetings with the landholders and their attorneys were held to address their concerns. The final lack of regulatory authority for the FEN did not trouble the project designers or agency representatives, because they understood from the start that the project would go forward as a public–private partnership. The property rights issue, however, was an unanticipated inflammatory issue that consumed considerable time and effort for everyone involved (Carr 2002).

BIODIVERSITY DATA ISSUES AND PLANNING STRATEGIES

As described by Hoctor et al.,: "In the state of Florida the application of integrated reserve design principles has been forwarded since the 1980s as a means to effectively conserve biodiversity in the face of rapid human population growth and habitat fragmentation" (2000, 985). The university team relied largely on existing data that indicated important biodiversity areas for conservation when developing their DSM. In the late 1980s, the Florida Game and Fresh Water Fish Commission (FWC) now known as the Florida Fish and Wildlife Conservation Commission performed GAP analysis and viability assessments for a number of target or indicator species. Jim Cox and Randy Kautz conducted a study for the FWC in 1994 called "Closing the Gaps," which examined focal species—such as those species that have a wide range or those that may act as indicators for particular communities (Table 1.3).

These viability studies provided a good foundation for developing the FEN. In fact, they surpass the same type of studies for other states, even today, because the amount of information available for native species in Florida far exceeds that collected for native species in most other states (Hoctor, Carr, and Zwick 2000; Hoctor 2002). Additional data for the DSM came from the Natural Heritage Program now known as the Florida Natural Areas Inventory, including an analysis of aerial photos identifying areas of conservation interest. The main problem associated with data collection was currency; by the time remotely sensed land cover data had been thoroughly analyzed, they were often five or ten years out of date. This is an inherent problem with data used for GIS applications anywhere. Although the investigators used remotely sensed data from the late 1980s and early 1990s, they also used SPOT imagery from 1995–96 to identify newly developed areas and eliminate these from the study (Hoctor 2002).

The DSM included four steps: (1) identifying areas of ecological significance, (2) selecting hubs, (3) identifying linkages, and (4) creating the FEN by combining the identified hubs and linkages (Figure 6.2; Hoctor et al. 2004). A GIS process called least-cost path modeling was used to identify optimum linkages by identifying cost surfaces (also called "suitability surfaces" in the reports) and applying them to the ArcInfo GRID module. As a result of this analysis, 23 million acres (9.3 million hectares), or 57.5 percent of the state, are incorporated into the FEN. Of this amount, 11.8 million acres (4.8 million hectares) were within public lands, private preserves, or open water. Figure 6.3 illustrates the effects the greenway plan will have on a variety of ecological community types; those indicated will experience increased protection under the plan

The investigators believe that this method of protecting a majority of intact natural and seminatural landscapes may be a good coarse filter approach, although other conservation efforts are needed to adequately protect biodiversity within the state. Most rare natural communities and species in Florida are now represented in the FEN and existing conservation areas (Hoctor, Carr, and Zwick 2000). The university team notes that the process of prioritizing significant habitats and protecting a reserve system has been occurring in Florida for some time. The progress achieved through this project, however, is "the combination of a systematic landscape analysis of ecological significance and the identification of critical landscape linkages in a way that can be replicated, enhanced with new data, and applied at different scales" (Hoctor et al. 2004, 197).

POSTPROJECT EVALUATION

The Florida Greenways and Trails System was well received by the public largely because its high recreational and ecological values. The property concerns raised by private landowners damaged public acceptance of the project and pressured the FDEP and other state agencies to question the protection of such large tracts of land when development is so important to Florida's economy. However, it must be noted that the project has been fairly successful even in the face of such opposition, as shown by the private lands that appear on the final greenways maps. Most private property concerns have now been assuaged, and the idea of ecological connectivity and protection of large-scale landscape linkages has become codified as an important goal for most of Florida's land conservation programs (Carr 2002; Hoctor 2002).

The development of the five-year implementation plan did not signal the end of planning for ecological connectivity in Florida. Rather, it is an ongoing process that will be continually evaluated and revised. Some elements of this process include and update to the FEN, continued re-prioritization of lands for acquisition and protection, an annual identification of critical linkages, assessment of the process by various agencies, and the creation of new partnerships. The FGCC was mandated to create benchmarks by which they may measure the success of the project. These benchmarks, as described in *Connecting Florida's Communities with Greenways and Trails* (FDEP & FGCC 1998), are as follows:

1. Establish a connected system of greenways and trails from one end of Florida to the other. This system is measured in acres and miles.
2. Maintain resources within the greenways and trails so that these remain suitable for designation in the future.
3. Ensure that all Floridians are within a fifteen-minute commute to a greenway or trail.
4. Ensure that 95 percent of visitors to public-access greenways or trails are satisfied with their experience.

Future work is needed to maintain and protect the FEN. Individual species analysis is needed for the black bear (*Ursus americanus*) and Florida panther (*Puma concolor coryi*), two wide-ranging umbrella species that depend on large areas with high connectivity to survive and reproduce. Identification of core areas, corridors, and buffer zones is also needed (note that core areas are different than hubs; cores are managed areas, and hubs are unmanaged destinations). Increasing human development will also necessitate closing unnecessary roads in public areas, protecting high-priority land from conversion to intensive use, and avoiding major new road projects (Hoctor, Carr, and Zwick 2000). The team has already succeeded in proactively coordinating with the FDOT to place high-impact human uses in areas least disruptive to wildlife. In fact, the FDOT is working with Dan Smith a PhD student from the University of Florida Department of Wildlife Ecology and Conservation to determine where roads cross important elements of the FEN and what mitigation measures might be taken to reduce their impacts. The purpose of this research was to avoid critical areas and to decrease roadkill by building wildlife corridors and underpasses in appropriate locations (Hoctor 2002).

Several issues—primarily concerning data collection and analysis—that arose during this project are pertinent to all landscape architects who address biodiversity in their work. For example, although GIS is gaining momentum as an integral tool in landscape planning, it can prove to be too complex on several levels; at times, it may provide more detail than necessary or may fail to address the needs of the people who will be using the space after a plan is implemented. Also, the amount of time needed to amass, digitize, and rectify data using GIS may mean that the land use data relied on by a biodiversity planning project are no longer current. However, the usefulness of GIS in landscape planning—especially as a tool to map sensitive habitat and ecosystems—makes it worth addressing these problems. In fact, according to

Professor Carr, projects of this type and scale should not be undertaken without the use of GIS. This is becoming a reality for both governmental and private planning efforts, as GIS technology is quickly becoming more user friendly and data availability, accuracy, and currency are rapidly and continuously improving.

Species selection is another complicated data issue; no agreed-upon "best choice" method exists for determining which species or ecosystems require conservation efforts. Often, it is up to the landscape architect and consulting ecologist to make an educated decision about what is most important or integral in the specific area in question. The Florida Greenways Project uses both large, wide-ranging species and species of specific conservation interest to help define areas of ecological significance. For a project of this scale, this multispecies approach was appropriate.

Finally, the Florida Greenways Project shows that public involvement in projects that have an ecological component can provide useful insights as well as complications. For example, private landowners whose land was indicated to have high-priority status were not always willing to set this land aside for conservation purposes. On the other hand, citizen participation in the trail development process guided the team in a direction they did not expect to go—that is, they found it necessary to apply more weight to citizen experience and opinion than to the findings of a GIS model. This indicates that landscape architects need to be equally sensitive to both cultural and ecological values when working on projects that influence both types of systems. (Hoctor et al. 2004, 200), provide a basic solution for the difficulties that arise when planning for biodiversity:

> It has become clear that effective conservation of biodiversity and other natural resources will require a large scale, integrated and comprehensive approach that does not tread on private property rights. Integral to such an approach will be a combination of local participation and decision making that can build a conservation constituency with top down planning and oversight that comprehensively identifies ecological resources of statewide significance and promotes land use decisions that meet both local needs and protect the state's national heritage and ecological services.

Further, as Hoctor et al. (2004, 189) explain, the rationale behind using a landscape approach for a greenway project is that "a functional reserve network integral to effectively conserving Florida's biological diversity and other natural resources can be identified by using a landscape approach guided by regional conservation planning principles combined with information on areas needed to protect viable populations of target species and natural communities." It is important that the problem be addressed at multiple scales and from multiple perspectives, and that it provide for multiple functions, as much as is reasonably possible. This is true for large, statewide projects, such as the Florida Greenways Project, as well as for smaller projects. Often, it is the landscape architect who must bring together the divergent views of the parties involved to create a balanced, multiuse vision for the project.

CHAPTER 7

CONCLUSIONS AND DISCUSSION

Understanding biodiversity should be fundamental to landscape architects and planners because, by definition, most planning and design activities change spatial configurations, ecological patterns, and associated processes, often unintentionally. Our research found that biodiversity planning and design are most successful when integrated with other goals, including environmental education, environmental impact mitigation, and regulatory compliance. Landscape architects and planners are recognized for their abilities to synthesize and visualize complex information, their familiarity with construction processes, their skills in facilitating public participation, and their expertise in implementing and managing interdisciplinary projects. Our research also found that biodiversity is often important in broad-scale, public policy-related projects and when mandated by regulatory and permitting agencies.

Project and site-specific data are often too incomplete to explicitly support planning and design decisions—an inherent problem related to the site-and species-specific nature of the data required. Despite this common lack of good data for planning and design, monitoring has rarely been conducted, mostly because of cost and convenience limitations but also because of a general ignorance of the value of monitoring. This is unfortunate because it limits the ongoing involvement of landscape architects and planners in the projects they conceive, design, and build—and limits their ability to learn whether they achieved the intended results. This lack of monitoring causes missed opportunities (1) to contribute new knowledge to science, (2) to allow planners and designers to expand their interdisciplinary collaboration with scientists and decision makers, and (3) to develop and refine planning strategies and design responses that address biodiversity more effectively across a range of contexts and project types.

To become more active players, landscape architects and planners must become more familiar with the issues, terminology, and methods for biodiversity planning and design. They need to understand the complex issue of representative species selection and how to apply a selected method in the context of species or habitat associations and ecological models. The references included in this study provide a starting point. There may be a need to integrate this knowledge into landscape architecture education and to add to the requirements for professional licensure, linked in part to the rationale of protecting public health, safety, and welfare.

Including biodiversity protection as an additional objective to a project may also help landscape architects and planners garner a wider range of support and form partnerships that aid other efforts in landscape planning, such as water resource planning, agriculture and wood production, and community and cultural adhesion.

DISCUSSION OF CASE STUDY PROPOSITIONS

These five case studies were organized and conducted to address four general propositions related to biodiversity planning and design:

PROPOSITION 1.
Biodiversity planning is in demand in rural, suburban, and urban areas.

Is biodiversity chiefly an issue in remote areas, where human occupation and activities are minimized? Or is it a legitimate concern in cities and towns, where human activity predominates? The answer has important implications for the future role of landscape architects and planners in biodiversity planning and design. If biodiversity planning is in demand across the rural–urban continuum, it could represent an important, even unprecedented professional opportunity, suggesting a new branch of professional practice and an associated area of knowledge for education in landscape architecture and planning. In general, this study found that biodiversity planning is routinely integral to broad-scale landscape plans and is becoming more recognized in finer-scale landscape design projects.

Woodland Park Zoo, located within the city of Seattle, takes advantage of its mission to demonstrate biodiversity and educate the greater public in a highly urban context. The zoo is visited by more than two million visitors annually, holding a great potential to influence the public's understanding of, and appreciation for, biodiversity and its relation to habitat globally.

The Devens Federal Medical Prison is located in a rural–suburban area where strong public concern exists for environmental impacts, including biodiversity. The project's landscape architects recognized a special opportunity to introduce biodiversity opportunistically as a project goal, in part to help expedite the permitting and review process. The Devens project also demonstrated how a construction project can surpass the objective of merely minimizing its on-site impacts by restoring and increasing the quality and amount of habitat on site (i.e., a net gain) and also enhancing the habitat value of the watershed downstream.

Crosswinds Marsh linked an urban need (airport expansion) with a suburban–rural resource (Crosswinds Marsh site) and in the process satisfied a regional metropolitan need (county park). The project demonstrated how ex situ mitigation sites for urban construction projects can create significant opportunities in suburban and rural areas.

This large-scale mitigation project raises the ethical issue of the value of the wetlands created in comparison to those destroyed, regardless of the context of each. How is this success measured and for how long? And, perhaps more importantly, how can the lessons learned be communicated to others to benefit future projects?

The Willamette Alternative Futures Project addressed a wide range of planning issues in a major river basin that spans the urban to rural gradient. Like many regions of the United States, the basin is undergoing a fundamental economic change from an agricultural to a service-based economy. This shift is driving land use changes that have significant implications for biodiversity across the basin. As future scenarios of landscape conditions demonstrate, the region will lose biodiversity unless proactive planning strategies are put in place. The Willamette study uses biodiversity as a yardstick to measure the consequences of various alternative futures and to identify the best locations for protecting or restoring biodiversity aspart of alternatives future scenarios.

The Florida Greenways System spans the entire state and ranks biodiversity and recreational resources in rural, suburban, and urban contexts. Although most high-priority lands for biodiversity in the system were required to be at least 2,470 acres (1,000 hectares) in size, smaller, isolated priority areas were also identified and designated. Most of the high-priority areas for biodiversity conservation were in rural and remote locations, while the smaller priority areas were more often located in suburban and urban contexts. Linking the smaller urban and larger rural areas was the central innovative concept behind the statewide plan, as it is in much of greenway planning. This linkage concept integrates resources across the urban-rural continuum.

The case studies individually and collectively support the proposition that biodiversity is in demand across the urban–rural continuum. They also demonstrate the need for landscape architects and planners to understand the hierarchical nature of biodiversity across multiple scales, which provides the context in which biodiversity projects originate.

PROPOSITION 2.
Landscape architects and planners will play a larger role in biodiversity planning and restoration ecology as nondegraded habitat becomes scarce.

This proposition was designed to test the assumption that landscape architects can contribute significantly to biodiversity when restoration or habitat creation is needed or mandated. In these professional contexts, landscape architects bring particular expertise in construction and vegetation management.

Although a zoo cannot be considered a true restoration of habitat, exhibits can represent a type of habitat creation for a particular species (especially if designed according to the concept of landscape immersion) and may potentially lead to, and provide new knowledge for, the restoration of natural, wild habitats elsewhere.

The Crosswinds Marsh project was essentially an ecological restoration project; at the time it was built, it was the largest wetland mitigation project in the United States. The landscape architects led a large interdisciplinary team in developing new restoration concepts and actions to achieve project objectives. The undertaking also created an opportunity to expand the ecological mitigation requirements, adding public use and environmental education benefits.

The loss of rural land and the need to find ways to develop in a less destructive manner led to the involvement of University of Florida landscape architects in the Florida Greenways Plan. The landscape architects functioned as mediators between special-interest groups, including landowners, biologists, social scientists, and developers—each with focused agendas.

The Devens project—located on a former golf course on an U.S. Army post that contained a Superfund site—was essentially a restoration effort. Research has shown that protection, enhancement, and restoration of natural systems can provide the most cost-effective and ecologically sound techniques for stormwater management (Barrent 1997). Originally, the Federal Bureau of Prisons planned to build facilities on the entire 300-acre (121 hectare) parcel, until project designers developed a plan that reduced sprawl and preserved open space by organizing the facilities on 45 acres (18.2 hectares) of already-disturbed land.

The Willamette Alternative Futures Project demonstrated the causal links between alternative future possibilities and biodiversity and water quality. The models developed in the research will be used explicitly in ongoing riparian restoration efforts throughout the basin.

Overall, the case studies demonstrate how landscape architects can bring management skills to a project to integrate human needs with the needs of the environment for mutual benefits. The studies also show that when landscape architects become involved in projects on disturbed land, they have the capacity to solve aesthetic and environmental problems creatively while maximizing benefits to biodiversity. In these ways, landscape architects have important skills to contribute to the science and practice of restoration ecology.

PROPOSITION 3.
Biodiversity goals that are explicitly part of a project's mission or design process are more likely to be achieved.

This proposition addresses the relative importance of biodiversity in projects with multiple goals. When biodiversity is a primary goal, it should influence the entire project from conception through implementation. However, the project's impact on biodiversity can be assessed only through long-term monitoring.

Biodiversity was the fundamental goal of the long-range plan for Woodland Park Zoo. Zoos present a new frontier for the protection of biodiversity, although their role is often indirect. As David Hancocks (2001, 177) explained, zoos need to review their goals and philosophy. Zoo visitors should see and learn about species' interconnections within ecosystems. Zoos should aspire to make visitors aware of the central importance of biodiversity—even for human well-being.

In the Devens project, the biodiversity goal was secondary to the stormwater management objective. The fact that water quality improvement and habitat creation were primary goals from the outset ensured that the key hydrological aspects of the project were understood and designed in the broader context of biodiversity and restoration. However, because biodiversity was not an explicit project goal, it has not been systematically monitored since the project's completion, and therefore the project's impact on biodiversity remains speculative.

Crosswinds Marsh was a mandated wetland mitigation project with explicit biodiversity goals. The major wetland loss at the airport site set clear goals for the off-site wetland restoration, which structured all of the project's phases: assessment, planning, design, construction, and monitoring. Biodiversity considerations influenced every aspect of the project and produced much of the project's success—as verified through postproject monitoring.

The Willamette Alternative Futures Project centered on understanding and modeling the effects of urban growth on habitat and water quality. Since biodiversity concerns formed the core of the project, they are more likely to be incorporated into the work of other entities that use the project's data and recommendations. Therefore, biodiversity has a greater chance of being protected through planning at the river basin scale. The test will be (1) to evaluate the project's effect on public understanding and support for alternative planning strategies and (2) to monitor biodiversity comprehensively and over the long term.

Biodiversity was the tail that wagged the greenway dog in the Florida Greenways Plan. After the Florida Ecological Network was designed, it became the basis for integrating complementary goals, including hiking trails, recreation, and alternative transportation. At the time of this study, the ecological network was being implemented with biodiversity as an integral component.

Collectively, these cases demonstrate that when defined as a primary project goal, biodiversity is likely to remain predominant over other aspects and goals of the project. The studies reveal this trend through a variety of project types in different regions and contexts. The lesson is that biodiversity planning and design is a field of rapidly growing interest and often drives many projects that involve landscape architects and planners. The cases also demonstrate how landscape architects and planners are able to manage projects for multiple goals, adding value to biodiversity projects that is often key to the projects' acceptance, permitting, or funding.

PROPOSITION 4.

Integrating biological and ecological information with the planning and design process will contribute to a better balance between land use and the natural environment and will increase public awareness of biodiversity's value to humans.

This proposition seeks to learn the extent to which the case studies have influenced human–environment relationships and biodiversity awareness. We are asking whether planning and design professionals understand the magnitude and implications of biodiversity, and if so, what are they doing about it now? And what should they do about it in the future?

Through landscape immersion and cultural resonance, Woodland Park Zoo directly and explicitly increases human understanding and respect for the natural world and its animals. Zoos designed in this manner have been shown to increase human sympathy and lead to actions in support of animals in the wild.

The Devens stormwater project has caught the attention of design professionals, making them more aware of how stormwater mitigation projects can opportunistically enhance wildlife habitat. In addition, the project has already served as a model for other development activities at the larger Devens site. Anecdotally, the workers encountered at the federal medical prison facility during the case study visit seem interested in wildlife and have learned firsthand the potential for aquatic habitat restoration at the site.

Crosswinds Marsh illustrates the distinct potential landscape architects have to create a more constructive order between land use and human environment. The marsh now functions as a viable habitat for many species and communities and enhances human appreciation for wildlife through its public use component.

Through robust, data-verified modeling, the Willamette Alternative Futures Project demonstrated that habitat loss or degradation caused by urbanization negatively affects population levels and species health. If the diversity and viability of animal species are viewed as broad indicators of environmental condition, the project implies that human health and welfare would suffer if current trends were to continue or if conservation planning policies were relaxed. Since a primary focus of the project was to provide sound, defensible data for regional and local planning authorities, it will be telling to watch how the findings will be used to guide planning within the Willamette River Basin. Already, several other planning entities, including the Oregon Department of Transportation and the Federal Highway Administration, have incorporated findings of the project into their work.

The Florida Statewide Greenways Project shows that a rapidly growing state can make biodiversity protection a planning priority and can integrate biodiversity with multipurpose statewide planning. The ultimate test of this project's effectiveness will be through long-term monitoring of land use change, amount of land in conservation status, integration of recreation with conservation, and gamma-level biodiversity.

Biodiversity is profoundly important to humanity. In its broadest sense, biodiversity involves all forms of life and the processes and functions on which life depends. Paradoxically, although we as humans are dependent on biodiversity for our very existence, we are also directly responsible for an unprecedented global decline in biodiversity. Clearly, important work remains to be done. The American Society of Landscape Architects' habitat policy, the American Planning Association's Code of Professional Ethics, and the mission statement of the Society for Ecological Restoration each articulates the value and importance of integrating ecological information and knowledge into projects that can influence understanding and appreciation of biodiversity. The case studies reviewed provide strong evidence that landscape architects and planners are already significantly involved in this important work.

HOW CAN LANDSCAPE ARCHITECTS AND PLANNERS ADDRESS BIODIVERSITY IN THEIR WORK?

Human actions may negatively influence biodiversity in three main ways: causing habitat loss or fragmentation, introducing invasive species, and inducing global climate changes. All can be directly or indirectly influenced by decisions made by landscape architects and planners. In *Linkages in the Landscape*, a publication of the World Conservation Programme's Forest Conservation Programme, Bennett (1999) suggests four basic strategies for planning and designing for biodiversity:

1. Expanding the area of protected habitat
2. Maximizing the quality of existing habitat
3. Minimizing the impact from surrounding land use
4. Promoting connectivity of natural habitat to counter the effects of isolation.

While acknowledging the benefits of all four strategies, promoting connectivity as a synergistic action receives the highest priority. Bennett (1999, 156) states: "The distinctive role of connectivity in a conservation strategy is to 'tie together' habitats into a linked system to restore the natural flow and interchange of plants and animals across the landscape." Connectivity is defined as the "degree to which landscape facilitates or impedes movement among resource patches" (Bennett 1999, 8). Linkages have a variety of purposes, including acting as suitable habitat and as areas of flow for both resources (water, nutrients) and animals. Daily, migratory, dispersal, and range extension movements can all be aided by the presence of linkages, making them a useful tool for designers.

Linkages can be categorized into three types: (1) habitat corridors, which assist movement through inhospitable environments via continuous connections; (2) stepping stones, which are remnant patches that allow species to make short movements through disturbed habitat; and (3) habitat mosaics, which are places where the different states of vegetation are not well defined and there is a blending along the edges. Corridors are most appropriate for animals that move on the ground and organisms that cannot move through environments different from their own (e.g., reptiles and amphibians that cannot cross roadways). The different types of habitat corridors include natural corridors (stream valleys), residual linkages (fencerows in agricultural areas), regenerated corridors (abandoned railways), planted corridors (hedgerows), and disturbance corridors (transmission lines and roadsides). Stepping stones are most appropriate for flying organisms, particularly migratory birds. These may be a chain of natural patches (wetlands), small remnant patches (areas of unlogged forest within a clear-cut area), or patches that are human in origin (urban parks) (Bennett 1999; Hudson and Defenders of Wildlife 1991; Forman 1995).

Woodland Park Zoo does not provide habitat linkages in part because of its urban location, but also because of its function as a zoological garden. The Devens stormwater and wetland project could have addressed linkages by coordinating and integrating its plans with the nearby Oxbow National Wildlife Refuge, however linkages were not a part of the project scope and were not actively addressed in project planning or design. Crosswinds Marsh deliberately restricted hydrological linkages to the site to avoid invasive fish species from entering the site from downstream areas. Crosswinds has not been involved with a broader scale upland habitat linkage plan in the project vicinity. The Willamette Alternative Future Project addressed habitat connectivity through the coupling of the simple habitat types method with the PATCH model for a selected set of species. The Florida Greenways project addressed habitat connectivity explicitly, as a primary goal of the project, and through multiple steps in the planning process.

Linkages may have some negative aspects; in some cases, their connectivity may promote the spread of invasive organisms, diseases, and fire as well as increase breeding between subspecies. Also, landscape architects and planners should be careful to justify the use of linkages with their knowledge of current ecological principles as they relate to biodiversity. As Bennett (1999, 127) writes:

> Claims such as "wildlife corridor" or "animal movement corridors" should not be included or accepted in planning strategies unless consideration is given to the specific biological purpose of the linkage and how its design, dimensions and management will be directed to meet that goal. The risk of a loose acceptance of what constitutes a "wildlife corridor" is twofold: it is wasteful of land and resources if the objectives have little chance of being achieved, and it devalues the concept and legitimate need for landscape connectivity in conservation.

Groves's "Four-R Framework" provides an ecologically sound underpinning for a system of conservation lands. According to this framework, conservation lands should be representative, resilient, redundant, and restorative (Groves 2003, 30). A conservation system should be representative of the diversity within a landscape or region. To be sustainable over time, the system must be resilient to human and natural disturbances. As a buffer from stochastic events, a system should include redundancy. Finally, in highly fragmented landscapes, a conservation system may need to rely on restoration to include certain ecosystems.

Another caution is a change in focus from protecting biodiversity to providing multipurpose space for human activity, such as recreation and scenic appreciation, which could ultimately decrease the amount of protection provided for the species using the linkage(s). Designers and planners should ask such questions as:

- Where are the species—in patch edges or interior habitat?
- When are they sensitive to disturbance—seasonally or related to life cycle?
- What strategies exist to manage conflicts—segregating activities in space or in time?

As long as these ecological considerations are addressed, true multiuse areas of protection can be created. The Trails and Greenways Clearinghouse lists the following reasons to create multiuse trails and greenways areas (Rails to Trails Conservancy 2002):

- To preserve and create open spaces
- To encourage healthy lifestyles
- To increase opportunities for recreation
- To increase opportunities for nonmotorized transportation
- To strengthen local economies
- To protect the environment
- To preserve historically and culturally valuable resources.

Indirectly, greenways may further affect biodiversity by improving air quality through an increase in the use of alternative modes of transportation (biking and walking).

Restoration represents an important opportunity for landscape architects and planners. Conservation biology's subfield of restoration ecology has grown rapidly in recent years. Restoration ecology deals with both biodiversity conservation concerns and landscape issues, indicating a need for well-informed landscape architects and planners. Most scientists agree that it is always better to preserve intact habitats proactively rather than try to restore them. According to authors James MacMahon and Karen Holl in their essay "Ecological Restoration: A Key to Conservation Biology's Future" (2001), the future of conservation biology essentially rests on restoration techniques. MacMahon and Holl warn: "More land is being altered at an ever-increasing rate in the world than at any time in the past. This suggests that to 'conserve' anything will require restoration at some level" (254). The authors identify and present research concerning several key themes beneath the umbrella heading of restoration ecology. They list recovery processes, species introduction, scale, monitoring, using succession as a model for addressing restoration issues, and addressing policy as the key issues affecting the field. To become actively involved, landscape architects and planners must familiarize themselves with these aspects of landscape ecology.

Although many overlapping activities fall under the category of restoration ecology—including rehabilitation, reclamation, re-creation, ecological recovery, and designer landscapes—all require modification of the landscape on some level. Whether through reestablishing entire floral and faunal assemblages or through creating designer landscapes comprising unusual combinations of elements intended to provide habitat for a target species, the opportunity exists for landscape architecture and planning to figure prominently in biodiversity conservation by working more directly in the field of restoration ecology.

Currently, reliable information about the effectiveness of various restoration approaches is lacking. We hope that the projected growth of the field in the upcoming decade will produce more high-quality data about successful approaches to restoring habitats. This should stimulate a demand for professions involved in designing and manipulating landscapes. Already, several creative methods for funding and encouraging the use of restoration techniques have emerged. One such plan is the U.S. Fish and Wildlife Service's Partners for Fish and Wildlife Program, which offers matching funds for private landowners who implement restoration projects on their land.

Although many tools are available to landscape architects and planners addressing biodiversity in their work, it is important to understand that biodiversity can be viewed on different scales and therefore, as Sheila Peck (1998) notes, that it is important to also plan for biodiversity at a variety of scales. Generally, diversity is constrained by attributes of the hierarchical level above it, and it exhibits properties that can be described by the level below it. Biological and spatial scales are related but not necessarily equivalent. For example, levels of biological hierarchy may cover a wide range of sizes—the area covered by a population of large mammals (such as bears) dwarfs the area occupied by some insect populations. Biologists recognize the importance of understanding and planning for biodiversity at alpha, beta, and gamma scales (Groves 2003).

A link exists between spatial and temporal scales inasmuch as large areas experience slower changes and smaller areas experience more rapid change. Human-dominated landscapes, however, often do not follow this space-time correlation. Practitioners need to understand both the context and spatial scale or scales of their work as well as the many timescales their work is likely to influence.

The use of landscape linkages is an example of applying spatial scales (which range from project to landscape to regional levels) to planning and design. At the project level, linkages can be created with hedgerows, streams, or underpasses. At the landscape level, linkages exist as rivers or floodplain corridors or as broad reserve links. Finally, at the regional level, major rivers and mountain ranges can act as linkages (Bennett 1999).

Landscape architects and planners should specifically address biodiversity at all four levels of the biological hierarchy, when appropriate, because each level affects different aspects of diversity. The *landscape* scale is important because it is affected by both biotic and abiotic factors, ecological processes, and interactions between types of habitat patches. By focusing on the landscape scale, it is possible to protect a variety of known and unknown communities. The *community* scale is important because it allows designers and planners to pay more attention to detail, especially the different forms in which communities and ecosystems occur. It is at this scale that important species—such as keystone species, vulnerable or rare, endemic species and specialists—can be protected. Ecological processes are also important at the community scale, especially disturbance processes. At the *population* scale, landscape architecture should strive to maintain adequate habitat area while taking into account demographic, environmental, and genetic factors. Additionally, patterns such as metapopulation configurations and the distribution of populations throughout a species range need to be explicitly understood. Finally, landscape architects should acknowledge the *genetic* scale because genetic diversity increases the chances that a population will survive environmental changes over time (Peck 1998).

Landscape architects and planners should be knowledgeable about changes that occur in the landscape over both long and short time frames. Long-term changes generally consist of geologic and climatic processes (e.g., soil development, disturbance patterns), which can be influenced by landscape architects only over the very long term but that should still be considered because they affect biodiversity. Short-term changes—such as fluctuations in predator–prey relationships or occurrences of fire—affect the structure and dynamics of communities. These changes can be influenced by human disruptions, which can interrupt fire regimes, modify water or wind patterns, and introduce diseases, pollution, and fragmentation. Landscape architects and planners should be aware of the effects of human disturbance and learn to employ strategies that provide extra protection to the biodiversity of communities and populations (Peck 1998).

Biodiversity not only represents an important opportunity for planning and design professionals but also presents great ethical and technical challenges. A professional crosses an ethical line when skills are used to help construct projects in rare or threatened ecosystems or habitats. We agree that our professional societies and associations should adopt more explicit ethical rules to guide professional practice. Professionals need to appreciate the differences among mitigation, restoration, replication, and habitat creation, and they need to practice accordingly, guided by an ethic based on sustainability and stewardship—to learn when to "just say no" to habitat destruction in the name of mitigation.

Design and planning professionals should rise to new challenges: (1) to collaborate as equal partners with scientists not only to solve biodiversity challenges in projects but to contribute to policy that can influence broad regions; (2) to add critical project-based data to the knowledge base through systematic monitoring and evaluation; and (3) to turn the tide on biodiversity decline, one project and one plan at a time.

LAF ACKNOWLEDGMENTS

Support for the *Land and Community Design Case Study Series* is provided by the JJR Research Fund, which supports applied research that explores the complex interrelationship of social, physical, economic and environmental forces that comprise sustainable design and development; the CLASS Fund Ralph Hudson Environmental Fellowship, which supports research in landscape change, preservation and stewardship, and the connection between people and landscapes; and the AILA Yamagami Hope Fellowship.

The American Society of Landscape Architects, whose mission is "to lead, to educate, and to participate in the careful stewardship, wise planning, and artful design of our cultural and natural environments," is a leading contributor, providing ongoing generous support to LAF and its programs.

Major support for Landscape Architecture Foundation is provided by Landscape Forms; *Landscape Architect and Specifier News*; Design Workshop; EDAW; HNTB Corporation; The HOK Planning Group; L. M. Scofield Company; Landscape Structures; ONA; and Peridian International.

Lead donors include Burton Landscape Architecture Studio; The Eastlake Company; EDSA; NUVIS; Peter Walker & Partners; Scott Byron and Company; the SWA Group; ah'be landscape architects; Robert F. Bristol, FASLA; Carol R. Johnson Associates; Gentile, Holloway, O'Mahoney & Associates; Graham Landscape Architecture; Hughes, Good, O'Leary & Ryan; Reed Hilderbrand Associates; and Ten Eyck Landscape Architects.

The list of additional donors who provide generous and sustained funding is too lengthy to include, but their support is valued and essential to Landscape Architecture Foundation's programs.

GLOSSARY

Bioclimatic zones: world habitats that are defined by climate and vegetation. The Holdridge system, the basis for the bioclimatic zone presentation theme at the Woodland Park Zoo, classifies zones based on three parameters: temperature, precipitation, and evapotranspiration. These three parameters can be visualized as the three vertices of a triangle; a particular life zone is determined by its position in this triangle. One climax community typically exists within each life zone. Examples include tropical forest, savanna, temperate deciduous forest, and taiga.

Biodiversity: the totality—over time—of genes, species, and ecosystems, including the ecosystem structure and function that support and sustain life.

Bioengineering: an approach to stream bank and slope stabilization using native species planted in rolls and mats to produce rapid establishment and soil stabilization.

Biological hierarchy—levels of biodiversity scales: landscape, community, population, and genetic. These scales represent a range based on area, but also imply more complexity, including ecosystems and people, at the broader landscape and community scales.

Charismatic species: target species that are aesthetically appealing and likely to generate popular interest and support for conservation. Such species include butterflies (*Lepidoptera* spp.), gray wolves (*Canis lupis*), giant pandas (*Ailuropoda melanoleuca*), and orchids (family Orchidae).

Coarse filter approach: an approach that focuses on the patterns of larger areas, where the differences between map size and actual size is substantial (see Forman 1995). This approach generally uses habitat associations based on knowledge of species' habitat needs and preferences and remotely sensed vegetation data classified into communities. An example is GAP analysis.

Connectivity: the level of actual, or functional, connectivity in a landscape to support species habitat and movement. A high degree of connectivity helps both resources (water and nutrients) and animals move through a landscape.

Cultural resonance: a zoo design concept that builds on landscape immersion to show zoo visitors how animals and humans interact. Presenting zoo visitors with integrated examples of human and animal cultures reveals the human–natural world relationship.

Decision support model: a geographic information systems model based on raster data analysis. An example is that used by the University of Florida to delineate a physical plan for the Florida Statewide Greenway System (see University of Florida 1999).

Ecological community: an assemblage of species that exist together in the same areas and whose life processes are potentially interrelated.

Economically valuable species: those target species that are needed by local consumers or that hold value in the commercial marketplace. An example is the caribou (*Rangifer tarandus*), which is used by native hunters for food and clothing.

Ecoregion: a broad region of land or water that includes a distinctive assemblage of natural communities containing many of the same ecological processes and species, existing under similar environmental conditions, and depending on ecological interactions for long-term survival.

Ecosystem diversity: includes the number of species in a particular location, the ecological functions of the species, the variation in species composition within a region, the associations of species in particular areas, and the processes within and among the ecosystems. It also extends to the landscape and biome level.

Edge species: species that thrive along the perimeter of habitat patches, where two different landscape types abut. These species tend to be generalists.

EPT monitoring: systematic observations of the richness and referenced condition of invertebrate species of the orders Ephemeroptera (mayfly), Plecoptera (stonefly), and Trichoptera (caddisfly) in a given water body. It is a tool used to monitor the aquatic conditions in streams and rivers.

Endangered species: as defined by the Endangered Species Act of 1973, a species "in danger of extinction within the foreseeable future throughout all or a significant portion of its range" (U.S. Fish and Wildlife Service1988). Together with threatened species, endangered species comprise what are commonly referred to as federally listed species.

Endemic species: those species found only in a single location in the world.

Federally listed species: both endangered species and threatened species as listed under the Endangered Species Act of 1973.

Fine filter approach: an approach focusing on a smaller area that contains greater detail than a larger area (see Forman 1995). The term also refers to an approach of biodiversity assessment and planning focused on endangered species in which the specific habitat locations are known and mapped. It is often used in combination with the coarse filter approach.

Fish index of biotic integrity: an index of overall integrity of fish in a given water body as compared with historic, reference levels. It is a tool used to measure the aquatic conditions in streams and rivers.

Flagship species: those target species that are popular and charismatic. They attract popular support for conservation and often help to spearhead a conservation effort in a particular landscape. Vertebrate species, such as the spotted owl (*Strix occidentalis*) in the Pacific Northwest or the Florida panther (*Puma concolor coryi*), are often considered flagship species.

Floristic quality index (FQI): a composite index used to aid quantitative comparisons, or rankings, of plant communities among different sites associated with restoration, management, or long-term monitoring. The FQI is based on a species list with coefficients of conservatism (C) ranging from 0 to 10 assigned for plant species by local or regional experts. C values of 0 or 1 are given to species adapted to severe disturbance, 2 or 3 for degraded but more stable communities, 4 to 6 for commonly occurring matrix species, 7 or 8 for moderately degraded natural areas, and 9 or 10 for high-quality natural areas.

Focal species: those species whose requirements for persistence include attributes that must be present for a landscape to meet the needs of most of the species in the given area. This is essentially an extension of the umbrella species concept. When dealing with multispecies management, biologists group species according to threats and then select the most sensitive species for each threat to act as the focal species. This species then determines maximum acceptable levels of threat. An example is the hooded robin (*Melanodryas cucullata*) in Australia, which is sensitive to forest fragmentation.

Fragmentation: the breaking up of a habitat, ecosystem, or land use type into smaller parcels, or habitat patches.

GAP analysis: an approach (the National Gap Analysis Program, or GAP), conducted by the Biological Resource Division of the U.S. Geological Survey, used to identify how well native animal species and natural communities are represented in lands that are currently conserved. Gaps are areas where species or communities, or both, are not adequately represented. Focusing on more "ordinary" species, it is essentially an offshoot of the hotspot approach; in this case, both ecological processes and species distribution are examined to determine which areas should receive protection before they become vulnerable. Vegetation is mapped using satellite images, and potential, or expected distributions of native animal species are mapped using museum or agency specimen collection records, known general ranges, and affiliations with the mapped vegetation. The resulting geographic information system maps are then overlaid with maps of land management areas in order to focus conservation efforts. Gap analysis is a coarse filter approach to biodiversity assessment and planning.

Generalists: species that can survive in a variety of habitat types and often on a variety of food sources. In contrast to specialist species, they tend to fare well in fragmented landscapes with a high ratio of edge habitat.

Genetic diversity: the variation of genes within species, including separate populations of the same species or genetic disparity within populations.

Greenway: as defined by the Florida Statewide Greenways Project, "a corridor of protected open space that is managed for conservation and/or recreation." Such corridors cross a variety of landscapes (rural to urban), are generally linear in shape, and have a many other diverse characteristics (public versus privately owned, wide versus narrow, green versus blue). Most importantly, greenways emphasize connectivity. (See Ahern 2002 and University of Florida 1999.)

Habitat corridor: a landscape linkage that assists movement through inhospitable environments using continuous connections. A habitat corridor is most appropriate for nonflying terrestrial species or species that have difficulty crossing heterogeneous landscapes. The many different types of habitat corridors include natural corridors, residual linkages, regenerated corridors, planted corridors, and disturbance corridors.

Habitat mosaic: a place where the different states of vegetation are not well defined and a blending occurs along the edges.

Hierarchy theory: a theory that stresses the importance of examining the landscape as a system of interconnected elements that can be viewed on a variety of scales to understand processes and trends at any one scale. Each element functions as a unit. Larger scales provide stability, while smaller scales provide variation.

Hotspot: an area in the landscape that supports an especially high degree of biodiversity. An example of a hot spot would be patches of tropical rain forest with high biodiversity.

Indicator species: species used to signal changes in the health of a given ecosystem and of other species within that system. Indicators may be positive, in that they are expected to correlate positively with ecological integrity or biodiversity, or negative, in that their presence indicates degrading ecosystem health. Indicators are used as part of a proactive strategy to anticipate problems before they occur.

Island biogeography theory: a theory developed by Robert MacArthur and Edward Wilson (1967) to explain the size effect of patches on biodiversity. The theory is derived from observations of populations on small oceanic islands. Following the formation of an island, a period of colonizations and extinctions ensues until equilibrium of species diversity is reached. Island area, isolation, and age are the major limits on colonization and extinction. Island biography theory has been extrapolated to understand the dynamics of terrestrial landscapes with habitat patches that may be fragmented or isolated into a spatial pattern analogous to some oceanic islands.

Keystone species: those species whose impact on ecosystems is disproportionately large relative to their abundance. They often function in close association with landscape processes and disturbances. One example is the beaver (Castor canadensis), whose engineering effects on the landscape are integral to shaping ecosystems.

Landscape immersion: the illusion for zoo visitors that no barriers exist between themselves and the animals. This impression is accomplished by bringing the exhibit plantings out into the human viewing areas, thereby extending the character of the life zone; by strategically controlling viewpoints so that the animals appear to be in a large, natural environment; and by concealing barriers as much as possible. Landscape immersion makes Woodland Park Zoo, for example, different from other conventional zoos that rely on obvious barriers to separate the captured animals from zoo visitors. This technique creates a sense of empathy to see an animal in its "natural" environment rather than behind a high fence or concrete wall.

Linkage: an element of the landscape that provides connectivity between large habitat patches. Several types of linkages exist, including habitat corridors, stepping stone habitats, and mosaic habitats. They can have both positive and negative effects. Positive effects include increasing the mobility of organisms that might not be able to cross unfamiliar habitat and providing an area of unimpeded flow for water. Negative effects include the spread of disease, insects, or fire. Linkages may also act as trails for human use.

Metapopulation theory: a theory first proposed by Richard Levins in 1970. Metapopulations are populations of a species that reside in many relatively small and spatially isolated patches of habitat that at times suffer local extinctions only to be replenished by populations in other patches. Alone, these populations would be highly susceptible to permanent extinction, but taken together, they constitute viable populations, capable of withstanding and recovering from local extinctions over time.

Mosaic: a collection of landscape patches, corridors, and matrix that together form a heterogeneous pattern (Forman 1995).

Nature Conservancy conservation status rank: a conservation status ranking system developed by the Nature Conservancy and the Natural Heritage Network. It functions on a 1 to 5 scale, with species in categories GX to G3 considered at risk.

- GX—presumed extinct
- GH—possibly extinct
- G1—critically imperiled (five or fewer occurrences or fewer than one thousand individuals)
- G2—imperiled (between six and twenty occurrences or between one and three thousand individuals)
- G3—vulnerable (twenty-one to one hundred occurrences or between three and ten thousand individuals)
- G4—apparently secure (some cause for long-term concern; more than one hundred occurrences or more than ten thousand individuals)
- G5—secure (widespread and abundant)

Patch: a nonlinear landscape area that is fairly homogeneous and is distinct from the surrounding landscape (Forman 1995).

PATCH model (Program to Assist in Tracking Critical Habitat): a biological modeling tool that incorporates the effects of habitat quality, quantity, and pattern on species life history parameters, such as survival rates, fecundity, and migration. The PATCH model diagrams where wildlife species should occur and at what densities they can be expected to viably exist. PATCH highlights landscape connectivity implications for wildlife.

Proactive strategies: conservation and assessment efforts undertaken before a problem arises or before a problem is beyond mitigation. An example is the National Gap Analysis Program.

Reactive strategies: conservation and assessment efforts undertaken after a problem or issue has been identified. These are strategies of preserving biodiversity that focus on preserving specific endangered species or that try to restore degraded or lost habitat. The endangered species approach is an example.

Restoration ecology: the reestablishment or rehabilitation of entire floral and faunal assemblages and their supporting physical infrastructure, including landform and hydrology.

Species richness: the number of species in a given area.

Species area theory: a theory (offered by MacArthur and Wilson in 1967) predicting that a 90 percent reduction in habitat area results in a loss of half of the total species in that area.

Species at risk: those species categorized under The Nature Conservancy conservation status ranking system as GX (presumed extinct), GH (possibly extinct), G1 (critically imperiled), G2 (imperiled), or G3 (vulnerable).

Species diversity: the variety of species within a region. Species diversity can be measured in many ways; however, the number of species in an area—species richness—is often used. Species diversity is also thought of in terms of "taxonomic diversity," which considers the relationship of one species to another.

Species guild: a group of target species that use a particular resource in similar ways. One example is all the bird species that make their nests in holes in tree trunks—e.g., cavity nesting species, such as the American kestrel (*Falco sparverius*), barred owl (*Strix varia*), hairy woodpecker (*Picoides villosus*), and Eastern bluebird (*Sialia sialis*), among others.

Stakeholders: the people who have a concern in a particular decision, either as individuals or as members or representatives of a group. Stakeholders include people who influence a decision, such as government officials, as well as those affected by the decision, such as citizens living in a particular area involved in the issue or action being considered.

Stepping stone habitat: a type of landscape linkage made up of remnant patches that allow species to make short movements through disturbed habitat. This type of habitat is most appropriate for birds and other organisms that fly.

Target species: indicator species that are chosen as targets for conservation priorities. These are often chosen more for their value in conservation politics than for their validity as true biological indicators.

Threatened species: a principal status category under the Endangered Species Act of 1973, threatened species are defined as "those animals and plants likely to become endangered within the foreseeable future throughout all or a significant potion of their ranges" (U.S. Fish and Wildlife Service 1988). Together with endangered species, they comprise "federally listed" species.

Umbrella species: target species that require large areas of habitat to maintain viable populations. Protecting these species' habitat protects the habitat and populations of numerous other species within the range, like an umbrella. Because they tend to function as coarse filters, focusing on these species is an efficient means of meeting the needs of many species without having to monitor every individual species. Examples include the grizzly bear (*Ursus arctos*) and the American bison (*Bison bison*).

Urban growth boundaries (UGB): a zone around a city. Development is allowed inside the line, whereas only very limited development is allowed outside the line. Most UGBs are updated periodically to accommodate growth pressures.

Vulnerable species: species that are in danger of going extinct. When the U.S. government recognizes a species' vulnerability because of its advanced state, that species is considered to be threatened or endangered. An example is the bald eagle (*Haliaeetus leucocephalus*).

BIBLIOGRAPHY

Ahern, J. 1995. Greenways as a planning strategy. *Landscape and Urban Planning* 33 (1–3): 131–55.

——— 2002. Greenways as Strategic Landscape Planning: Theory and Application. Wagenrugen University, Netherlands.

All Taxa Biodiversity Inventory. 2002. The role of ATBI's in the global biodiversity crisis: Notes from the Great Smokies. http://www.discoverlifeinamerica.org/atbi/ (accessed July 18, 2006).

American Planning Association. 1992. Ethical principles in planning. http://www.planning.org/ethics/ethics.html (accessed July 18, 2006).

American Society of Landscape Architects. 2000. ASLA code of environmental ethics. http://www.asla.org/about/codeenv.htm (accessed July 18, 2006).

Arendt, R. 1999. *Growing greener: Putting conservation into local plans and ordinances.* Washington, DC: Island Press.

Askins, R. A. 2002. *Restoring North America's birds: Lessons from landscape ecology.* New Haven, CT: Yale University Press.

Baker, J. (ecologist, U.S. Environmental Protection Agency). 2002. Interview by Jack Ahern. January 10. Corvallis, OR.

Baker, J. P., D. W. Hulse, S. V. Gregory, D. White, J. Van Sickle, P. A. Berger, D. Dole, and N. Schumaker. 2004. Alternative futures for the Willamette River Basin, Oregon. *Ecological Applications* 14 (2): 313–24.

Baker, J. P., and D. H. Landers. 2004. Invited feature introduction. *Ecological Applications* 14 (2): 311–12.

Barrent, K. R. 1997. Introduction to ecological engineering for water resources: The benefits of collaborating with nature. Paper presented at the annual conference of the New England Water Environment Association.

Bastasch, R., S. Gregory, and S. Vickerman. 2002. Interview by Jack Ahern. January 10. Corvallis, OR.

Bauer, D. (wetland manager, Wayne County Parks, Crosswinds Marsh). 2001. Interview by Jack Ahern. December 20. New Boston, MI.

Beatley, T. 1994. *Habitat conservation planning: Endangered species and urban growth.* Austin: University of Texas Press.

Benfield, F. K., M. D. Raimi, and D.D.T. Chen. 1999. *Once there were greenfields: How urban sprawl is undermining America's environment, economy, and social fabric.* New York: Natural Resources Defense Council.

Bennett, A. F. 1999. *Linkages in the landscape: The role of corridors and connectivity in wildlife conservation.* Gland, Switzerland: IUCN–The World Conservation Union.

Berlein, J. 2002. Interview by Jack Ahern. January 8. Woodland Park Zoo, Seattle.

Bioengineering Group/W. Goldsmith. 2002. Interview by Jack Ahern, Elizabeth Leduc, and Mary Lee York. January 15. Carol R. Johnson and Associates, Boston, MA.

Boyd, J., and L. Wainger. 2002. Measuring ecosystem service benefits for wetland mitigation. *National Wetlands Newsletter* (Environmental Law Institute) (November–December): 1, 11–15.

Bridgeman, J. 2002. Interview by Jack Ahern. January 8. Jones & Jones, Seattle.

Brown, K. S., Jr., and G. G. Brown. 1992. Habitat alteration and species loss in Brazilian forests. In *Tropical deforestation and species extinction,* ed. T. C. Whitmore and J. A. Sayer, 119–42. London: Chapman and Hall.

Carol R. Johnson Associates—R. Sorenson, J. Amodeo, and C. Cogswell. 2002. Interview by Jack Ahern, Elizabeth Leduc, and Mary Lee York. January 15. Carol R. Johnson and Associates, Boston, MA, and Devens Federal Prison site, Devens, MA.

Carol R. Johnson Ecological Services. 1995. Application for a programmatic general permit Federal Medical Center Complex, Fort Devens, Massachusetts and application for water quality certificate Federal Medical Center Complex, Fort Devens, Massachusetts. Boston, MA: U.S. Department of Justice, Federal Bureau of Prisons.

Carr, M. H. 2002. Telephone interview by Jack Ahern, Elizabeth Leduc, and Mary Lee York. January 17. University of Massachusetts, Amherst.

Clay, G., ed. 1980. Woodland Park Zoological Gardens: President's Award of Excellence. *Landscape Architecture,* September.

Conservation International. 2002. Conservation strategies: Hotspots. http://www.conservation.org/xp/CIWEB/home# (accessed July 18, 2006).

Cox, J. and R. Kautz. 1994. *Closing the Gap.* Tallahassee, FL: U.S. Fish and Wildlife Service.

Croonquist, M. J., and R. P. Brooks. 1991. Use of avian and mammalian guilds as indicators of cumulative impacts in riparian wetland areas. *Environmental Management* 15 (5): 701–14.

Dahl, T. E. 2000. *National Wetlands Inventory.* St. Petersburg, FL: U.S. Fish and Wildlife Service.

Dennison, D. L. 2000. Crosswinds Marsh wetland mitigation. *Land and Water* (November/December): 23–27.

———(vice president, SmithGroup JJR). 2001. Interview by Jack Ahern. December 19. SmithGroup JJR, Ann Arbor, MI.

Devens Enterprise Commission Regulatory Authority. 1999. Wetlands Protection. http://unixweb.choiceone.net/d/e/devensec.com/cgi-bin/showz.cgi/l/decregs406.html (accessed July 18, 2006).

Dinerstein, E., G. Powell, D. Olson, E. Wikramanayake, R. Abell, C. Loucks, E. Underwood, et al. 2000. *A workbook for conducting biological assessments and developing biodiversity visions for ecoregion-based conservation. Part I: Terrestrial ecoregions.* Washington, DC: Conservation Science Program, World Wildlife Fund–USA.

Drake, J. A., H. A. Mooney, F. di Castri, R. H. Groves, F. J. Kruger, M. Rejmanek, and M. Williamson, eds. 1989. *Biological invasions: A global perspective.* New York: John Wiley and Sons.

Ehrlich, P. R. 1988. The loss of diversity: Causes and consequences. In *Biodiversity,* ed. E. O. Wilson and F. M. Peter, 3–18. Washington, DC: National Academy Press.

Ehrlich, P. R., and E. O. Wilson. 1991. Biodiversity studies: Science and policy. *Science* 253:758–62.

Environmental Defense and the Texas Center for Policy Studies. 2003. Texas environmental profiles—Wetlands: Essential habitats. http://www.texasep.org/html/wld/wld_swet.html (accessed July 18, 2006).

Erwin, T. L. 1982. Tropical rainforests: Their richness in *Coleoptera* and other arthropod species. *Coleoptera Bulletin* 36:74–75.

Evanoff, P. (project landscape architect, SmithGroup JJR). 2001. Interview by Jack Ahern. December 19 and 20. SmithGroup JJR, Ann Arbor, MI.

Feinsinger, P. 2001. *Designing field studies for biodiversity conservation.* Washington, DC: Island Press.

Fleishman, E., D. Murphy, and P. F. Brussard. 2000. A new method for selection of umbrella species for conservation planning. *Ecological Applications* 10 (2): 569–79.

Flink, C., R. Searns, and L. Schwartz. 1993. *Greenways: A guide to planning, design, and development.* Washington, DC: Island Press.

Florida Department of Environmental Protection and Florida Greenways Coordinating Council (FDEP & FGCC). 1998. *Connecting Florida's communities with greenways and trails: The 5-year implementation plan for the Florida Greenways and Trail System.* Tallahassee: Florida Department of Environmental Protection.

Forman, R.T.T. 1995. *Land mosaics: The ecology of landscapes and regions.* Cambridge: Cambridge University Press.

Forman, R.T.T., D. Speirling, J. A. Bissonette, A. P. Clevenger, C. D. Cutshall, V. H. Dale, L. Fahrig, R. France, C.R. Goldman, K. Heaure, J.A. Janes, F.J. Swanson, T. Turentine, and T.C. Winter. 2003. *Road ecology: Science and solutions.* Washington, DC: Island Press.

Francis, M. 2001. A case study method for landscape architecture. *Landscape Journal* 20 (1): 15–29.

———. 2003a. *Urban open space: Designing for user needs.* Land and Community Design Case Study Series. Washington, DC: Island Press and Landscape Architecture Foundation.

———. 2003b. *Village Homes: A community by design.* Land and Community Design Case Study Series. Washington, DC: Island Press and Landscape Architecture Foundation.

Freudenberger, D. 1999. *Guidelines for enhancing grassy woodlands for the Vegetation Investment Project.* Canberra, Australia: Commonwealth Scientific and Industrial Research Organisation (CSIRO) Wildlife and Ecology.

Gibbs, W. W. 2001. On the termination of species. *Scientific American* 285:40–49.

Goldsmith, W., and K. R. Barrett. 1998. Bioengineered system in existing stream channel. Paper presented at the American Society of Civil Engineers Wetlands Engineering and River Restoration conference, March 22–27, Denver.

Groves, C. R. 2003. *Drafting a conservation blueprint: A practitioner's guide to planning for biodiversity.* Washington, DC: Island Press.

Groves, C. R., L. S. Kutner, D. M. Stoms, M. P. Murray, J. M. Scott, M. Schafale, A. S. Weakley, and R. L. Pressey. 2000. Owning up to our responsibilities: Who owns lands important for biodiversity? In *Precious heritage: The status of biodiversity in the United States,* ed. B. A. Stein, L. S. Kutner, and J. S. Adams, 275–300. Oxford: Oxford University Press.

Hammond, P. M. 1995. The current magnitude of biodiversity. In *Global biodiversity assessment,* ed. V. H. Heywood and R. T. Watson, 113–38. Cambridge: Cambridge University Press for United Nations Environment Programme.

Hancocks, D. 2001. *A different nature: The paradoxical world of zoos and their uncertain future.* Berkeley: University of California Press.

Herman, K. D., L. A. Master, M. R. Penskar, A. A. Reznicek, G. G. Wilhelm, and W. Brodowicz. 1996. *Floristic quality assessment with wetland categories and computer application programs for the state of Michigan.* Lansing: Michigan Department of Natural Resources, Wildlife Division, National Heritage Program.

Heywood, V. H., G. M. Mace, R. M. May, and S. N. Stuart. 1994. Uncertainties about extinction rates. *Nature* 368:105.

Heywood, V. H., and R. T. Watson. eds. 1995. *Global biodiversity assessment.* Cambridge: Cambridge University Press for the United Nations Environment Programme.

Hilty, J. A., and A. Merenlender. 2000. Faunal indicator taxa selection for monitoring ecosystem health. *Biological Conservation* 92:185–97.

Hoctor, T. S. 2002. Telephone interview by Jack Ahern, Elizabeth Leduc, and Mary Lee York. January 17, University of Massachusetts, Amherst.

Hoctor, T. S, M. H. Carr, and P. D. Zwick. 2000. Identifying a linked reserve system using a regional landscape approach: The Florida Ecological Network. *Conservation Biology* 14 (4): 984–1000.

Hoctor, T. S., M. H. Carr, P. D. Zwick, and D. S. Maehr. 2004. Florida Statewide Greenways System Planning Project: its realization and political context. In *Ecological networks and greenways,* ed. R. Jongman and G. Pungetti, 222–50. Cambridge: Cambridge University Press.

Hoctor, T. S., J. Teisinger, M. Carr, and P. Zwick. 2001. *Ecological Greenways Network prioritization for the State of Florida.* Tallahassee, FL: Office of Greenways and Trails.

Hudson, W. E., and Defenders of Wildlife. 1991. *Landscape linkages and biodiversity.* Washington, DC: Island Press.

Hulse, D. 2000. Land conversion and the production of wealth. *Ecological Applications* 10 (3): 679–82.

———. 2002. Interview by Jack Ahern. January 11. Eugene and Corvallis, OR.

Hulse, D., J. Eilers, K. Freemark, C. Hummon, and D. White. 2000. Planning alternative future landscapes in Oregon: Evaluating effects on water quality and biodiversity. *Landscape Journal* 19 (1–2): 1–19.

Hulse, D., S. Gregory, and J. Baker, eds. 2002. *Willamette River Planning Basin atlas: Trajectories of environmental and ecological change.* 2nd ed. Corvallis: Oregon State University Press.

Hulse, D. W., A. Branscomb, and S. G. Payne. 2004. Envisioning alternatives: Using citizen guidance to map future land and water use. *Ecological Applications* 14 (2): 325–41.

Hypner, J. (vice president, Barton Malow Construction Services, Detroit). 2001. Interview by Jack Ahern. December 19. Detroit Metropolitan Airport, Detroit, MI.

Jennings, M. D. 2000. Gap analysis: Concepts, methods and recent results. *Landscape Ecology* 15:5–20.

Johnson Johnson & Roy/Inc. 1991. *Detroit Metropolitan Wayne County Airport Wetland Mitigation Plan.* Ann Arbor, MI: Johnson Johnson & Roy/Inc.

———. 1999. *1998 Wetland Mitigation Monitoring Report: Detroit Metropolitan Wayne County Airport.* Ann Arbor, MI: Johnson Johnson & Roy/Inc.

Jones, G. 1982. Design principles for preservation of animals and nature. In the proceedings of the American Association of Zoological Parks and Aquariums 1982 annual conference, Phoenix.

———. 1989. Beyond landscape immersion to cultural resonance: In the Thai elephant forest at Woodland Park Zoo. In the proceedings of the American Association of Zoological Parks and Aquariums 1989 annual conference, Pittsburgh.

———. 2002. Interview by Jack Ahern. January 7. Jones & Jones, Seattle.

Jones, J. P. 2002. Interview by Jack Ahern. January 8. Jones & Jones, Seattle.

Jones & Jones. 1976. *Woodland Park Zoo: Long range plan, development guidelines, and exhibit scenarios.* Seattle: Department of Parks and Recreation.

Keystone Center. 1991. Final consensus report of the Keystone Policy Dialogue on Biological Diversity on Federal Lands 1991. http://ceres.ca.gov/ceres/calweb/biodiversity/def_KC.html (accessed July 18, 2006).

Kittredge, A. M., and T. F. O'Shea. 1999. Forestry practices on wildlife management areas. *Massachusetts Wildlife* 49:33–38.

Kitzhaber, J. 2000. Analysis: How Portland, Oregon, utilizes urban environmentalism to help make the city more livable. Interview by J. Williams. July 27. Live broadcast, *Talk of the Nation*, National Public Radio.

Lambeck, R. J. 1997. Focal species: A multi-species umbrella for nature conservation. *Conservation Biology* 11 (4): 849–56.

Landres, P. B. 1983. Use of the guild concept in environmental impact assessment. *Environmental Management* 7:393–98.

Landre, P. B., Verner J., J.W. Thomas. Ecological Uses of Vertebrate Indicator Species: A Critique. *Conservation Biology*. 1988. (2) 1-13.

Lawrence Halprin and Associates. 1972. *The Willamette Valley: Choices for the future.* Executive Department, State of Oregon. Available at: http://willametteexplorersinfo/publication/ (accessed August 28, 2006).

Lecesse, M. 1996. Little marsh on the prairie. *Landscape Architecture* 86 (7): 50, 52–55.

Leopold, A. 1949. *A Sand County almanac and sketches here and there.* New York: Oxford University Press.

Levins, R. 1970. *Extinction: Some mathematical questions in biology.* Vol. 2. Providence, RI: American Mathematical Society.

Little, C. 1995. *Greenways for America.* Baltimore, MD: Johns Hopkins University Press.

Lomborg, Bjørn. 2001. *The Skeptical Environmentalist: Measuring the Real State of the World.* Cambridge: Cambridge University Press.

Lovejoy, T. E. 1980. A projection of species extinctions. In *Council on Environmental Quality (CEQ): The Global 2000 Report to the President,* vol. 2, 328–31. Washington, DC: U.S. Government Printing Office.

Mac, M. J., P. A. Opler, C.E.P. Haecker, and P. D. Doran. 1998. *Status and trends of the nation's biological resources.* 2 vols. Reston, VA: U.S. Department of the Interior, U.S. Geological Survey.

MacArthur, R. H., and E. O. Wilson. 1967. *The theory of island biogeography.* Princeton, NJ: Princeton University Press.

MacMahon, J. A., and K. D. Holl. 2001. Ecological restoration: A key to conservation biology's future. In *Research priorities in conservation biology,* ed. M. E. Soulé and G. Orians, 245–69. Washington, DC: Island Press.

Mandala Collaborative/Wallace McHarg Roberts and Todd (WMRT). 1975. *Pardisan.* Philadelphia: WMRT.

Martin, F. E. 2000. Where the runway ends: Crosswinds Marsh heals the land while raising environmental awareness. *Landscape Architecture* 90 (7): 26–31, 82–83.

Massachusetts Executive Office of Environmental Affairs, Division of Fisheries and Wildlife Natural Heritage and Endangered Species Program. 2001. *BioMap: Guiding land conservation for biodiversity in Massachusetts.* Boston: Executive Office of Environmental Affairs.

Massachusetts Nature Heritage and Endangered Species Program. 1994. *Atlas of Estimated Habitats of State-listed Rare Wetlands Wildlife.* Massachusettes Division of Fisheries and Wildlife, Boston.

Master, L. L., B. A. Stein, L. S. Kutner, and G. A. Hammerson. 2000. Vanishing assets: Conservation status of U.S. species. In *Precious heritage: The status of biodiversity in the United States,* ed. B. A. Stein, L. S. Kutner, and J. S. Adams. Oxford: Oxford University Press.

Mawdsley, N. A., and N. E. Stork. 1995. Species extinctions in insects: Ecological and biogeographical considerations. In *Insects in a changing environment,* ed. R. Harrington and N. E. Stork, 322–69. London: Academic Press.

May, R. M. 1988. How many species are there on Earth? *Science* 241:1441–49.

McHarg, I. L. 1996. *Quest for life.* New York: John Wiley.

McPeek, M. A., and T. E. Miller. 1996. Evolutionary biology and community ecology. *Ecology* 77:1319–20.

Michigan Department of Natural Resources. 1991. Permit 90-14-1320. Issued to Wayne County Division of Airports. August 8.

Miller, K. R., J. Fortado, C. De Klemm, J. A. McNeely, N. Myers, M. E. Soulé, and M. C. Trexler. 1985. Issues on the preservation of biological diversity. In *The global possible,* ed. R. Repetto, 337–62. New Haven, CT: Yale University Press.

National Biological Information Infrastructure (NBII). 2003. Biodiversity definitions. http://www.nbii.gov/issues/biodiversity (accessed September 6, 2004).

Noss, R. F. 1991. Indicators for monitoring biodiversity: A hierarchical approach. *Conservation Biology* 4 (4): 355–64.

Noss, R. F., and A. Y. Cooperrider. 1994. *Saving nature's legacy: Protecting and restoring biodiversity.* Washington, DC: Island Press.

Organisation for Economic Co-operation and Development (OECD). 2002. *Handbook of biodiversity valuation: A guide for policymakers.* Paris: OECD.

Ott, S. A. (vice president, SmithGroup JJR). 2001. Interview by Jack Ahern. December 19 and 20. SmithGroup JJR, Ann Arbor, MI.

Owens-Viani, L. 2002. Ripple effect. *Landscape Architecture* 92 (8): 88–89.

Pacific Northwest Ecosystem Management Consortium [now called the Pacific Northwest Ecosystem Research Consortium]. 2002. Home page. http://www.orst.edu/dept/pnw-erc/ (accessed July 18, 2006).

Paulson, D. R. 2002. Interview by Jack Ahern. January 9. Slater Museum of Natural History, Tacoma, WA.

———. N.d. *Woodland Park Zoo ecologist's report: World bioclimatic zones.* Seattle.

Peck, S. 1998. *Planning for biodiversity: Issues and examples.* Washington, DC: Island Press.

Pollock, M. M., R. J. Naiman, and T. A. Hanley. 1998. Plant species richness in riparian wetlands: A test of biodiversity theory. *Ecology* 79 (1): 94–105.

Power, M. E., D. Tilman, J. A. Estes, B. A. Menge, W. J. Bond, L. I. Millis, G. Daily, J. C. Castilla, J. Lubchenco, and R. T. Paine. 1996. Challenges in the quest for keystones. *Bioscience* 46:609–20.

Pryor, T. (manager, Oxbow National Wildlife Refuge). 2002. Telephone interview by Mary Lee York. January 14. University of Massachusetts, Amherst.

Rails to Trails Conservancy. 2002. Trails and Greenways Clearinghouse. http://www.trailsandgreenways.org/ (accessed July 18, 2006).

RAMSAR. 2003. The Ramsar Convention on Wetlands: Wetlands and Biodiversity. Available from World Wide Web: http://www.ramsar.org/about/about_biodiversity.htm (accessed July 18, 2006).

Raven, P. H. 1988. Our diminishing tropical forests. In *Biodiversity,* ed. E. O. Wilson and F. M. Peter, 119–22. Washington, DC: National Academy Press.

Risser, P. 2002. Interview by Jack Ahern. January 11, 2002. Corvallis, OR.

Schneider, K. 2003. *The Paris–Lexington road: Community-based planning and context sensitive highway design.* Land and Community Design Case Study Series. Washington, DC: Island Press and Landscape Architecture Foundation.

Schrader-Frechette, K. S., and E. D. McCoy. 1993. *Method in ecology: Strategies for conservation.* Cambridge: Cambridge University Press.

Schumaker, N. H., T. Ernst, D. White, J. Baker, and P. Haggerty. 2004. Projecting wildlife responses to alternative future landscapes in Oregon's Willamette Basin. *Ecological Applications* 14 (2): 381–400.

Scott, J. M., F. Davis, B. Csuti, R. Noss, B. Butterfield, C. Groves, H. Anderson, S. Caicco, F. Derchia, T. C. Edwards, et al. 1993. Gap analysis: A geographic approach to protection of biological diversity. *Wildlife Monographs* 123:1–41.

Shannon, C. E., and W. Weaver. 1949. *The mathematical theory of communication.* Urbana: University of Illinois Press.

Simberloff, D. 1998. Flagships, umbrellas, and keystones: Is single-species management passé in the landscape era? *Biological Conservation* 83 (3): 247–57.

Sipple, W. S. 2002. Wetland functions and values. http://www.epa.gov/watertrain/wetlands/index.htm (accessed July 18, 2006).

Smith, F. D. M., R. M. May, R. Pellew, T. H. Johnson, and K. S. Walter. 1993. Estimating extinction rates. *Nature* 364:494–96.

Society for Ecological Restoration International. 2004. Mission statement. http://www.ser.org/about.asp (accessed July 18, 2006).

Species 2000. 2002. Home page. http://www.sp2000.org/ (accessed July 18, 2006).

Stein, B. A., L. S. Kutner, and J. S. Adams, eds. 2000. *Precious heritage: The status of biodiversity in the United States.* Oxford: Oxford University Press.

Storch, I., and J. A. Bissonette. 2003. *Landscape ecology and resource management: Linking theory with practice.* Washington, DC: Island Press.

Stork, N. E. 1999. The magnitude of global biodiversity and its decline in the living planet. In *Crisis biodiversity science and policy,* ed. J. Cracraft and F. T. Grifo, 3–32. New York: Columbia University Press.

Thompson, J. W. 1999. Stormwater unchained: outside a Massachusetts prison, bioengineered detention ponds turn runoff into an asset. *Landscape Architecture* 89 (8): 44–51.

Thompson, J. W., and K. Sorvig. 2000. *Sustainable landscape construction: A guide to green building outdoors.* Washington, DC: Island Press.

University of Florida, Department of Landscape Architecture. 1999. *Phase II: University of Florida Statewide Greenways System Planning Project recommendations for the physical design of a statewide greenway system.* Final report. Gainesville: University of Florida, Department of Landscape Architecture.

U.S. Department of Agriculture. 1997. *Agricultural resources and environmental indicators, 1996–1997.* Agricultural handbook no. 712. Washington, DC: U.S. Government Printing Office.

U.S. Department of Fish and Wildlife, Endangered Species Program. 2002. Environmental Conservation Online System (ECOS). http://ecos.fws.gov/ecos/index.do (accessed July 18, 2006).

U.S. Environmental Protection Agency. 2000. *Applicability of biodiversity indices to FKCCS species and ecosystems region 5, USEPA, Chicago United States Army Corps of Engineers, Jacksonville District, 2000.* http://www.saj.usace.army.mil/projects/biodivind2ndrev.htm (accessed July 18, 2006).

U.S. Fish and Wildlife Service (USFWS). 1988. Endangered Species Act of 1973, as Amended through the 100th Congress. Washington, DC: U.S. Department of the Interior, USFWS.

———. 1997. *Status and trends of wetlands in the conterminous United States 1986–1997.* http://training.fws.gov/library/Pubs9/wetlands86-97_lowres.pdf (accessed July 18, 2006).

Van Sickle, J., J. Baker, A. Herlihy, P. Bayley, S. Gregory, P. Haggerty, L. Ashkenas, and J. Li. 2004. Projecting the biological condition of streams under alternative scenarios of human land use. *Ecological Applications* 14 (2): 368–80.

Vitousek, P. M. 1988. Diversity and biological invasions of oceanic islands. In *Biodiversity,* ed. E. O. Wilson and F. M. Peter, 181–89. Washington, DC: National Academy Press.

Washington Transcript Service. 1998. William Cohen, secretary of defense holds news conference on base closings. April. Washington Transcript Service.

Weitz, J., and T. Moore. 1998. Development inside urban growth boundaries: Oregon's empirical evidence of contiguous urban form. *Journal of the American Planning Association* 64 (4): 424–40.

White House, Office of the Press Secretary. 1999. Economic renewal: community reuse of former military bases. Press release, April 21. http://clinton6.nara.gov/1999/04/1999-04-21-report-on-community-reuse-of-former-military-bases.html (accessed June 4, 2006).

Whittaker, R. H. 1975. *Communities and ecosystems.* 2nd ed. New York: Macmillan.

Wilcove, D. 1993. Getting ahead of the extinction curve. *Ecological Applications* 3:218–20.

Wilcove, D. S., D. Rothsein, J. Dubow, A. Phillips, and E. Losos. 2000. Leading threats to biodiversity: What's imperiling U.S. species? In *Precious heritage: The status of biodiversity in the United States,* ed. B. A. Stein, L. S. Kutner, and J. S. Adams, 275–300. Oxford: Oxford University Press.

Wilcox, B. A. 1982. In situ conservation of genetic resources: Determinants of minimum area requirements. In *National parks, conservation and development: The role of protected areas in sustaining society,* ed. J. A. McNeely and K. R. Miller, 639–47. Proceeding of the World Congress on National Parks, Bali, Indonesia, October 11–12, 1982. Washington, DC: Smithsonian Institution Press.

Willamette Partnership. 2005. Home page. http://clev17.com/~willamet/?q= (accessed August 22, 2006).

Willamette Riverkeeper. 2002. Home page. http://www.willamette-riverkeeper.org (accessed July 18, 2006).

Willamette Valley Livability Forum. 2001. Home page. http://www.lcog.org/wvlf/ (accessed July 18, 2006).

Wilson, E. O. 1988. The current state of biological diversity. In *Biodiversity,* ed. E. O. Wilson and F. M. Peter, 3–18. Washington, DC: National Academy Press.

World Conservation Union–IUCN. 2000. News: Confirming the global extinction crisis, a call for international action as the most authoritative global assessment of species loss is released. IUCN-World Conservation Red list Program. http://www.iucn.org/en/news/archive/archive2000.htm (accessed July 18, 2006).

World Conservation Union–IUCN, Species Survival Commission. 2001. The SSC Red List Programme. Home page. http://www.redlist.org/info/programme.html (accessed July 18, 2006).

World Resources Institute (WRI). 1992. *Global Biodiversity Strategy: Guidelines for action to save, study, and use Earth's biotic wealth sustainably and equitably.* World Resources Institute, Washington, IUCN and UNEP.

World Zoo Organization. 1993. *The World Zoo conservation strategy executive summary.* Chicago: Chicago Zoological Society.

Yin, R. K. 1994. *Case study research: Design and methods.* Thousand Oaks, CA: Sage.

Zedler, J. B. 1996. Ecological issues in wetland mitigation: An introduction to the forum (in wetland mitigation). *Ecological Applications* 6 (1): 33–37.

INDEX